## Advance Praise for
## *What Men Want to Say to Women (But Can't)*

"Part memoir, part cultural analysis, *What Men Want to Say to Women (But Can't)* offers a searing indictment of the lies told by feminism about what men and women want—and don't want. Drawing on her own experience of abuse, divorce, childrearing, and marriage, McAllister is a veritable second Shakespearean Kate, calling her sisters to cast off their shrewishness out of love for the fathers, husbands, brothers, and sons who love, serve, and protect them."

—Rachel Fulton Brown, Author of *Mary and the Art of Prayer: The Hours of the Virgin in Medieval Christian Life and Thought*, and *Milo Chronicles: Devotions, 2016-2019*

"Too much of conservative media has become similar to the Left media in terms of culture. Too much assimilation. Too much pack mentality. Too little critical thinking. Too few contrarians. Denise is part of a remnant still willing to say difficult things and ask uncomfortable questions. At the very least, hear her out to check your own thinking. Whether you agree or disagree, you'll be smarter for it."

—Steve Deace, Author of *Truth Bombs: Confronting the Lies Conservatives Believe (To Our Own Demise)* and Host of *Steve Deace Show*, BlazeTV

"*What Men Want to Say to Women (But Can't)* serves as a wake-up call for women to finally understand men. It blows the lid off the lies Americans have been sold about men and masculinity and helps modern women feel the kind of compassion and respect for men that most Americans used to share. Denise McAllister is a bold writer, which is precisely what this subject needs."

—Suzanne Venker, Author of *The Alpha Female's Guide to Men and Marriage*

"A triumph of compassion, insight, and good sense. Denise McAllister doesn't just want to fix how men and women talk to each other. She wants to heal a fraying holy sacrament. Read this book to save your marriage—or to find one."

—Milo Yiannopoulos

"Denise McAllister has no fear of controversy. Her ideas about men and women bristle some, but also speak for many who feel cowed in today's constricted public square. With fierce devotion to tradition, she tackles a world of gender that is changing at a breakneck pace and urges our society to pump the brakes."

—David Marcus, New York Correspondent
for *The Federalist*

"Sometimes a book comes along to articulate the inchoate insanity that leftist ideology has wreaked on human affairs. Denise McAllister's *What Men Want to Say to Women (But Can't)* is that book as the author outlines how 'woke' feminism and identity politics have distorted what women expect and what men can and cannot deliver in relationships. McAllister patiently unravels how women have been programmed to misunderstand the realities of relations between the sexes, and she's extremely clear-headed about how this strain of society-destroying cultural Marxism has been promulgated. This book will help bring everyone back to basic realities in how men think, so women can deal with them realistically."

—Lisa Schiffren, NYC-based writer on politics and culture
and Senior Fellow at Independent Women's Forum

# WHAT MEN WANT TO SAY TO WOMEN (BUT CAN'T)

DENISE McALLISTER

A BOMBARDIER BOOKS BOOK
An Imprint of Post Hill Press
ISBN: 978-1-64293-312-3
ISBN (eBook): 978-1-64293-313-0

What Men Want to Say to Women (But Can't)


Cover Photo by Michael McAllister

Post Hill Press
New York • Nashville
posthillpress.com

Published in the United States of America

*To Michael and Dad*

# CONTENTS

# ACKNOWLEDGMENTS

All books are a labor of love. This one was also a labor of perseverance. I couldn't have done it without the help of many people, beginning with my wonderful husband who has been a rock by my side through good times and bad. I still can't believe he loves me, but he seems to hang in there on this crazy ride we've taken together. He and our children have been the loves of my life, and I thank each of them for their constant support while writing this book.

I want to thank my mom, whose confidence in me never fails, whose prayers for me never cease, and whose love has sustained me through the darkest times of my life. She is a woman of strength—a true feminist of the first variety who has helped me become the woman I am today. Likewise, my dad has been an inspiration in writing this book, and stories about him grace the pages. He believes in me, and that faith has helped me to believe in myself. In the same way, my brother, Steve, has been a constant source of encouragement—a cheerleader, just as he has always been, from soccer games when I was young to the political theater I find myself in today.

I also want to acknowledge two amazing ladies who have encouraged me during this project by listening to me untangle the thoughts in my head and reading the manuscript. My best friend, Katelyn, has been a fellow soldier in the battle for masculinity, and she has supported me with her insight and intuition—my "Scottish fairy" who sprinkles me with magic every day. And my dear friend Jenni has been prayer warrior on my behalf as I've emailed her chapter after chapter, peppering her with questions and fishing for reassurances. Her faithfulness is humbling.

I'd also like to thank my publisher, David Bernstein, who bravely took on this controversial project and has stood beside me when others jumped ship. His brilliance has been a North Star, and I appreciate him for the strong man he is. Another man of strength who has inspired me to write this book is David Limbaugh. He has been a gentle voice of reason and faith along this journey, helping me to stay the course in the midst of turmoil—as has Lynda McLaughlin, a woman of unrelenting strength, honesty, and a take-no-prisoners attitude. She has motivated me to keep moving forward, reminding me to "just breathe."

Finally, I have to thank Jesus Christ, my savior and my God. Without him, I can do nothing. Only by his strength have I been able to ride the storm of life and not only survive, but thrive, in hope of helping others—however imperfectly. I pray this book will honor him and serve as a guidepost in human relations, reminding us of who we are and who we can become.

# INTRODUCTION

"If you're going to compete with men in the workplace, don't ask for special favors or entitlements when you fail—and, for God's sake, stop being so bitchy."

"No, you're not as physically strong as a man—and, if you think you are, take the hits of competition like a man."

"Stop telling me how to parent our children. I'm not you. I'm not a woman. Children need a man in their lives—their father."

"When I look at your boobs, I don't want to rape you. I just think you're beautiful—and sexy. That's not a threat. That's nature, and it's good."

These are just some things men want to say to women but can't—not without backlash or accusations of sexism. In this book, I unpack these sentiments—why men think them, why women should take them seriously, and how we can bridge fissures formed in relationships due to contemporary feminism. No matter one's political persuasion, most of us agree there's something deeply wrong in America today. Conflict has reached a fever pitch as our nation has become alarmingly polarized in the political arena. Many look to politicians and public policies for solutions, but journalist Andrew Breitbart rightly said that politics couldn't be fixed if culture is ignored, because "politics is downstream from culture." I would take this observation a step further—politics might be downstream from culture, but culture is downstream from relationships. If we don't focus on the personal building blocks of society, we will fail to fix problems in culture and the politics that flow from it. If relationships are sick or broken—especially those between men and women—then everything else is affected. If there's little love, respect, and trust there, you won't find it anywhere else.

Issues of sexuality have always been controversial, but they are more so today than at any time in modern history. I recognize the complexity of the subject and the varied presuppositions many bring to it, which is why I want to state up front that I'm presenting this book from a theistic worldview in general and a Christian perspective in particular, though my purpose is not to write a religious treatise with Scripture quotations as "proofs." Instead, I want to present a reasonable case from a cohesive worldview to aim for mutual understanding about masculinity and relationships.

Discussing anything regarding human nature without having a solid philosophical worldview and theological foundation is like running around in midair. We won't get anywhere because then our arguments are simply one fleeting subjective "truth" bouncing off another, which is the state of too much discourse in America today. My presupposition is theistic because it makes the most sense to me, and it has been established as reasonable throughout history. I ask that you hear it in that context and not as a pulpit in which dogma and doctrine are dictated. Ask yourself, "Do her arguments make sense?" If they do, even if you reject the religious premise, then we have a starting point of shared understanding. I echo what Thomas Sowell writes in the introduction to his book about another controversial topic—race: "If this book can contribute to understanding on a subject where misunderstandings abound, then it will have done its work."[1]

I have been a journalist for years, writing about cultural issues—including feminism and its relationship to masculinity. As I've gathered data on these topics, I've found them to be mixed as the soft sciences of sociology and psychology are woefully lacking in objectivity and often corrupted by confirmation bias. When it comes to human nature, some things can't be measured by an experiment. We have to experience them. We have to listen to the testimony of people about their own lives. But most of all, we have dig deep into fundamental truths to interpret the times in which we live. This is what I bring to you: experience, common sense, and philosophical, theological, and teleological truths—not random and conflicting "scientific" studies. To those who demand materialistic inquiry about relationships, sexuality, humanity, and identity, I wonder what they think of the countless books written before the modern era that imparted much wisdom about the human condition based on historical knowledge and philosophical understanding rather than faux science.

I am a woman talking to other women about men—and I know men. I've observed them in a variety of scenarios for over thirty years as a journalist. I have a father, a brother, a son, a stepson, male cousins, friends, and coworkers. I've been married twice. I grew up in a testosterone-laden world outside of Camp Lejeune, my youth impacted by the aftermath of the Vietnam War. I've worked in a "man's world," from advertising to news reporting, often the only woman in the room. I attended divinity school and often found myself in classes and ministry meetings surrounded by men. I've seen the worst of men and the best of men. I've seen men in moments of rage and in moments of profound gentleness. I've seen them excited like little boys as they unlock the secrets of how something works. I've seen tears in their eyes at the loss of a beloved dog or while watching a film that blew across a raw wound left by an absent father. I've felt the pain of their emotional backlash and cowered beneath a heavy hand. I've felt the comfort of their grace as I've lashed out in anger they did not deserve. I've witnessed their sacrifice in war and the faraway look in their eyes as they remember horrors I could never imagine. I've basked in the warm passion of a man's kiss and felt the strength of his body envelop mine. I've been chilled by a man's cold look in the face of betrayal and touched scars on their bodies taken for me. I've held them like a child in my arms and watched with delight as they held a child in their own. Tenderness, love, strength, and wonder. A man is a glory to behold, a power to respect, and a heart to treasure.

In an age in which men are not appreciated as they should be, I offer my insights and learning from the wisdom of other women and men themselves. I reach past the messages of the modern era and take from the knowledge of religious texts and philosophies, which have more insight into human nature and identity than the best of psychological theory today, to offer advice on how to repair damage done by modern feminism to relationships between men and women.

I stand not as a teacher above you or a dogmatic scold to intimidate you, but as a woman and fellow sojourner along life's winding and wondrous path. I'm encouraged in my approach to this work by C. S. Lewis. In his book *Reflections of the Psalms*, he confesses to his readers that he's no worldly "expert" on the topic, no historian or authority in an academic sense. He writes that he offers insight "for the unlearned about things in which I am unlearned myself." By way of analogy, he compares his communication with readers to two schoolboys figuring out a truth taught by their teacher, and it fits well with my own efforts.

> It often happens that two schoolboys can solve difficulties in their work for one another better than the master can. When you took a problem to

> the master, as we all remember, he was very likely to explain what you understood already, to add a great deal of information which you didn't want, and say nothing at all about the thing that was puzzling you. I have watched this from both sides of the net; for when, as a teacher myself, I have tried to answer questions brought me by pupils, I have sometimes, after a minute, seen that expression settle down on their faces which assured me that they were suffering exactly the same frustration which I had suffered from my own teachers. The fellow-pupil can help more than the master because he knows less. The difficulty we want him to explain is one he has recently met. The expert met it so long ago that he has forgotten. He sees the whole subject, by now, in such a different light that he cannot conceive what is really troubling the pupil; he sees a dozen other difficulties which ought to be troubling him but aren't.[2]

Too many experts on human sexuality have forgotten what they once knew, or they have never grasped truths perceived by common sense because they let their methods get in the way. Like Lewis, I write this book as someone on equal footing with you who has experience—both as a seasoned journalist and as a Christian apologist who worked in teaching ministry for years—to bring to the conversation.

Often those who delve into the subject of feminism approach it much in the same way as others in contemporary circles: talking about the progression of the feminist movement, explaining its origins, and analyzing its effect on women and, to some degree, men. But there is a cold detachment to many of these writings, pregnant with too much academic study and filled with deviations from the reality of the everyday person's life. Other publications on these issues are typically self-help in nature—valuable in their own right but not always insightful about the nature of the human heart and how the two sexes mysteriously join together, not just in marriage, but in all sorts of relationships. This is what I offer—a broader, deeper look at a troubling issue in today's culture.

In doing so, I don't assume to instruct women as a master—though, like Katherine in Shakespeare's *The Taming of the Shrew*, I will inevitably confront, rebuke, implore, and remind you of what you've forgotten or never considered. The iconic play tells the tale of a woman determined to live distinctly from a man, refusing to recognize her need of his strength or his need of her devotion. Its language no doubt makes the contemporary feminist ear burn, but the underlying message of appreciating men is as relevant today as it was then. The two sexes haven't changed much from the dawn of time, not at their core or according to their design—this, despite modern efforts to subvert it. The grueling march toward androgyny in the name of equality has sown discord rather than peace. It has robbed us of trust and lessened us more than enlightened us. It has weighed us down in unhappiness and loneliness. It has fueled hatred instead of fostering love. It has divided us instead of making us whole.

We need to change—not a revival of male-dominated social structures in which women are denied rights and recognition of their abilities, but a reawakening of our designed purposes as human beings, as men and women, and as distinct individuals (a cohesive construction of identity that I explore in detail in Chapter 9). We need to remember our true *selves*—that we are not self-created but objectively fashioned for a reason: to love others, to complement and help the opposite sex as faithful companions rather than as competitors, and to reflect God's image on earth in our work, our enjoyments, and our relationships to one another and the world. Our sexuality is not merely self-expression. It is rooted in the image of another, of God, who made us to have meaning and to carry out responsibilities in this life that cannot be separated from our distinctive natures as males and females. This objective reality doesn't mean we all act the same, fill the same roles, or share the same experiences in life. We are not cookie cutouts of an ideal. We are actual individuals with distinctive callings and abilities, but overarching that individuality is a shared purpose with every other human being on the planet to be threaded into the fabric of history as males and females, not as androgynistic distortions of reality. That purpose, again, is rooted in love, cooperation, and faithful reflection of God's goodness and objective truth in our lives.

In my criticism of feminists and the Marxist ideology that modern feminism has become, I am not referring to traditional feminism with all of its struggles to secure the rights and opportunities women enjoy today. I am addressing feminism as it is now—a power paradigm in which groups are pitted against others in the name of equity and individual rights are consumed by collectivist ideals. As I address these issues, I realize not all individuals fit into the same mold. But it is impossible to discuss such broad topics by addressing every outlier, every individual quirk, or even every personal experience, though I share some with you as way of connecting through narrative. My discussion deals in generalities about sexuality, though not abstracts, and they are credible because universals and archetypes are the bedrock of human existence, no matter the individual expressions. When I talk about women in general, I realize there are exceptions. Not everyone will see themselves in these descriptions, but they are common enough to induce confessions that they hit closer to home than we ordinarily care to admit.

Likewise, as I talk about men, I recognize that they are not all the same. There are good and bad men and a whole spectrum in between. When I praise men for the beautiful creatures they are, I am not excusing or glorifying abuse of any sort. I am communicating with sincere people about fundamental realities that are exemplified in lives well lived even if not perfectly executed. If your response is, "But what about all the bad guys?" you will miss the point. As Sowell said in similar discussions about race, "One cannot predict, much less forestall, all the clever misinterpretations that others might put on one's words. The most that can be done is alert honest people to the problem."[3]

## CHAPTER 1

# FEMINISM FATALE

*"Girls, girls! Wipe those frowns off your faces and stop rolling your eyes. This disrespectful stance toward the man who is your lord, your king, your governor tarnishes your beauty the way the frosts of winter blights the land."*

—Katherine, John Crowther's modern (No Fear) translation of Shakespeare's *The Taming of the Shrew*

Men have a lot to say to women but often can't. They're drowning in America today because one feminist wave after another has beat against masculinity, pressing it down under the weight of female demands and reshaping it into a bastardization that's contrary to its divine design. The assumption is that male privilege has exhausted its run, and men must be silenced so others can speak—their song has played for too long and another melody needs to resonate throughout America. The very essence of their masculinity has been targeted, called into question, and labeled as noxious to an "enlightened" society. The notion of "toxic masculinity" is now pervasive in our national conversation, from politics to religious institutions, from academia and movies to advertisements. Gillette is one example. The company recently produced an ad portraying men as thoughtless, unacceptably aggressive, and sexually abusive—simplistic dolts who knuckle-drag their way through life. Customers protested Gillette's message, insisting there's nothing toxic about "traditional masculinity." At first, Gillette stuck with its politically correct message, but it eventually shifted gears and started a new campaign that changed the company's focus from social issues to local heroes displaying traditionally masculine traits.[4]

Anyone can scan history with its various cultures and discover different "masculinities" that seem to bear little resemblance to one another: the hard-drinking machismo of Mediterranean cultures; the gang mindset of urban America that historically cuts across racial and ethnic lines; the oppressive male dominance of Middle Eastern theocracies; the quiet gentility of eighteenth-century America; the rough "redneck" cultures of northern Britain that migrated to America's southern regions; and the battle-hardened warriors of tribal societies throughout Africa that require boys to hunt and kill animals by age twelve to prove their manhood. Some tribal cultures have such bizarre initiatory standards of masculinity that they would be rightly characterized as sadistic and immoral by civilized standards. The characteristics of manliness certainly change across cultures and time, but underlying these differences are basic similarities and universals that distinguish men from women—man as protector, provider, procreator, and leader. These universal masculine archetypes are qualities of nature, not mere roles. They are infused into the very essence of manliness for the benefit of society.

Americans, however, live in a culture that seeks sameness of the two sexes, robbing them both of their unique design and completion of each other. The result has been disastrous. In the words of Alexis de Tocqueville, who warned of equality's perverted conflation with sameness, "It may readily be conceived, that by thus attempting to make one sex equal to the other, both are degraded; and from so preposterous a medley of the works of nature nothing could ever result but weak men and disorderly women."[5] American women of Tocqueville's time in the early nineteenth century escaped this degradation, even as they enjoyed many more equalities with men (though certainly not all) than their aristocratic European sisters. These American heroines often exhibited "masculine strength of understanding and a manly energy," Tocqueville observed, but they did not fail to "retain the manners of women, although they sometimes showed that they had the hearts and minds of men."[6] While political rights and equal opportunities were a distant reality, these women were on the path to equality without being debased by sameness.

## LET MEN BE MEN!

Modern feminism's manufactured androgyny has created an identity crisis for men. They're confused or at least frustrated about how they're supposed to act at work, what they're allowed to say, how they're expected to raise their children, and what it means to be a lover. Feminists, who have ironically set masculinity up as the standard by which they measure equality, have propelled women into competition instead of cooperation with men. Feminists today have demanded to be equally represented in traditionally male positions, even when they're not qualified. Until recently, men haven't been pressured to take on women's roles, though they have often done this out of necessity as single-income homes have transformed into double-income homes. Women were once satisfied with being included among the men in their traditional workspaces, given opportunities without obstacles of discrimination, and respected for the skills they brought to a variety of occupations. Now, feminists want men to shed their masculinity in favor of a more feminine identity, both in their roles and their behaviors.

Not only are men expected to respect a woman's rights and a woman's capabilities in the workplace (and rightly so), but they're also expected to communicate like women, manage like women, and govern like women. Instead of men being free to emote like men, they're told to join local male support groups to spill their feelings as women would and touch each other in nonsexual ways so they won't be as aggressive. By participating in "cuddle" groups, they're expected to learn to appreciate male physical touch without resorting to "homophobia." This new feminized paradigm is far beyond male bonding and beating of drums around a fire in Robert Bly fashion. Sexual identity has flipped. Women now tell men they should be more "emotionally intelligent," when what they really want is for men to be more emotionally expressive. Emotionality is not the same as emotional intelligence, which is the mark of a mature masculine man. Instead of respecting this difference, feminists demand that men reflect a feminized ideal even as women insist that they're the same as men. If men don't comply with these contradictory expectations and if they remain intransigent in their masculinity, they're labeled toxic. If men want to hang out and watch sports, share their deepest feelings only with the woman they have chosen to love, enjoy spending time with other guys doing "manly" things without women invading their space, express sexual attraction to beautiful women, or train their boys to wrestle and compete, then they're told they're bad for society. The presumption—or rather the assertion—is they must reconstruct their masculinity to be considered acceptable in this new and "improved" egalitarian society.

## EQUALITY DOESN'T MEAN WHAT A LOT OF WOMEN THINK IT MEANS.

How did we get to this point? Why deviate from equality to sameness in expectation even if not in practice? Why isn't it enough for women to freely achieve through unhindered opportunities and enjoy prospects afforded to their male counterparts, instead of demanding change in the very core of a man's sexual identity? In no way do I advocate returning to a society in which women are kept in domestic roles under social pressure and stigma, but the feminist movement has progressed beyond its original intent. The dogma now is not only should society open its doors to allow women to achieve—something we should all applaud—but men must also change who they are. Egalitarianism is the goal. This shift is a severe perversion of simply accepting women into the broader spheres of society. Pro-feminists—intellectuals, psychologists, and academics who support feminist ideology—want a fantasy that robs men of their identity and freedom by reconstructing them into something other than what they are. They are now defined by "others"—the very imposition feminists denounced as patriarchal tyranny.

The influx of women into masculine roles in the name of equality has pushed men to adapt. For the most part, men have done a pretty good job doing just that. They welcome women into the workforce, and they help at home. They volunteer to take on different roles because they love the women in their lives, and they have been sensitive to changes women have made since the early days of the sexual revolution. The American male should be praised for his cooperation and adaptation to difficult cultural transformations. Men have been open to working with women in this modern era, but equality failed to be enough for the feminist movement. Sameness and even superiority have replaced the once noble cause of equal rights and liberty for all.

Today's feminism is an ideology devoid of divine purpose. Instead, it is rooted in conflict and a subjective paradigm in which we all make our own "truth" in the struggle for power between the masculine and feminine. It feeds on pride instead of fostering humility. It is a movement of fear, not love, of isolating autonomy, not mutual dependence. In Shakespeare's play *The Taming of the Shrew*, Katherine admonishes her female companions for their pride and arrogant refusal to humble themselves in a relationship with a man—humility that, when correctly understood and applied, would reap great benefit to all. Her speech is still relevant today and is a delight to read in full:

> Girls, girls! Wipe those frowns off your faces and stop rolling your eyes. This disrespectful stance toward the man who is your lord, your king, your governor tarnishes your beauty the way the frosts of winter blights the land. It mars your reputations as whirlwinds shake fair buds. And in no sense is it fitting or attractive. An angry woman is like an agitated fountain—muddy, unpleasant, lacking in beauty. And in this condition, no one—however dry or thirsty he may be—will stoop to sip or touch one drop of it.
>
> Your husband is your lord, your life, your keeper, your head, your sovereign, one who cares for you and who, for your ease and comfort, commits his body to harsh labor both on land and sea. Long, stormy nights at seas he stays awake, by day he endures cold while you lie safe and warm, secure in your beds at home. And in exchange he seeks

no more from you but love, kind looks, and true obedience—too little payment for so great a debt.

A woman owes her husband the same loyalty a subject owes his king. And when she is peevish and perverse, sullen, sour, and disobedient to his honest wishes, what is she but a loathsome, war-like rebel and an ungrateful traitor to her loving lord? I am ashamed that women are so foolish as to declare war when they should plead on their knees for peace, that they seek authority, suprem-acy, and power when they are under an obligation to serve, love, and obey.

Why are our bodies soft and weak and smooth, unfit for toil and trouble in the world, if not so that our soft qualities and our hearts should agree with our external parts? Come, come, you weak, ungovernable worms! My spirit has been as proud as each of yours, my courage as great, and my reason perhaps even better suited to bandy words back and forth and exchange frown for frown.

But now I see our weapons are like straws, our strength like a straw's weakness, and our weakness past comparison, so that we seem to be the thing we most are not. Humble your pride, then, since it's useless, and place your hand beneath your hus-band's foot. As a gesture of my loyalty, my hand is ready if he cares to use it. May it bring him comfort.[7]

Admittedly, I wouldn't use such harsh words in talking directly to women today, though "ungovernable worms" is sometimes tempting, especially when I'm watching pink pussy hats fill streets in women's marches and signs smeared with love of self and hatred for men. But Katherine's monologue is relevant. It's an echo of times past, but much needed in today's world in which modern feminism has become unmoored from its original purpose: to create more political freedom and social opportunities for women. Instead of elevating women according to their design as females, feminism has degenerated into a war on men. The result has been catastrophic, as men who have already been struggling with maturing into manhood in this modern technological age find themselves burdened by the demands of a tyrannical feminism. As they've navigated through the last six decades of a new landscape in which women have become more entrenched in typically masculine roles, they feel lost. Men have managed well at adapting to the changes in culture, but they struggle with women's failure to adapt to those same changes.

Feminists blame men for their ills when often it's women themselves who have been unable to adapt to the very changes they demand. Instead of being satisfied with equality and the personal responsibilities that come with freedom, they desire equal outcomes, denying innate—and sometimes even biological—differences. This self-centeredness has caused women to become stuck in a narcissistic frame in which they think more of their own desires, their own successes, their own goals in life, and their own will to power, without giving much thought to what men need and how they are to relate to them in this new modern era. In this cauldron of pride and self-pity, women have brewed for themselves unhappiness, anxiety, and depression. They have lost the joy of being a helpmate. The wholeness they yearn for without even realizing it is found in relationships with men—not just erotically, but in friendship and social relations. We are at peace when we are connected to one another, but feminism has forged detachment and brokenness where there should be unity.

## IT'S TIME FOR WOMEN TO GROW UP, TO LEARN HOW TO LOVE.

The result of this push for sameness has had a deteriorating effect on both men and women, as they have failed to mature. Feminism has told women they can have anything they want. Seeking their own happiness has been the goal instead of learning to suffer through life, facing inequalities as human beings have done since the dawn of time, and finding humility in the journey. Their focus has been wrong, and it has dramatically damaged the relationship between men and women. They have simply forgotten how to love. In the movie *Shadowlands*, C. S. Lewis (played by Anthony Hopkins) talked about how difficult life can be, how we suffer, and how this is merely part of being human. Happiness is not always attained. Getting what we want is often rare. Life can be hard. It's often unfair. Chasing ideals instead of living in reality leads us to frustration and resentment. In observing these trials of life, Lewis said, "I'm not sure that God particularly wants us to be happy. I think he wants us to be able to love and be loved. He wants us to grow up."

It's time for women to grow up, and essential to that is loving men and treating them with respect, appreciation, and kindness. A woman plays a powerfully influential role in a man's life, not by validating his manhood—only men can do this for one another—but by complementing him and helping him in his journey to be his best. When he is beaten down, challenged at every turn, used, abused, neglected, and disrespected, he withdraws. Resentment builds. Loneliness and depression seep into every aspect of his life, and a great gulf opens between him and others, especially women. The two are cast alone on each side of the chasm wondering why they're so miserable.

In their book *King, Warrior, Magician Lover: Rediscovering the Archetypes of the Mature Masculine*, Robert Moore and Douglas Gillette observe that modern men are cast adrift, often alone as they struggle in a culture deprived of mature masculinity. Many, they write, fall by the wayside with no idea of what went wrong. "We just know we are anxious, unloved and unappreciated, often ashamed of being masculine. We just know that our creativity was attacked, belittled, and left holding the empty bag of our lost self-esteem. We cave in to a dog-eat-dog world, trying to keep our work and our relationships afloat, losing energy, or missing the mark."[8] The authors blame this masculine despair on a highly feminized culture and the vestiges of a pre-feminism society in which men didn't properly mature into manhood due to pathologies and material values created by the modern world. Post-World War II was a time when technology blossomed and worldly success in America became more of a focus than living according to God's loving, selfless, and spiritually-minded purpose for human beings. This materialistic frame of living took its toll on male-female relationships. Feminism was a reaction to that undeveloped masculinity, but it has gone too far, losing itself in its own immaturity as women fail to understand and live according to their supportive and loving purposes as women in their relationships with men.

## MEN DON'T NEED TO BE LIKE WOMEN TO BE HAPPY.

At a time when both men and women are unhappy like never before in American history, experts still place the blame on masculinity.

Women, they say, are unhappy because they haven't achieved equality with men. The "patriarchy," they claim, "still exists, keeping women down." There aren't enough female CEOs, women in government, or women in the military. Equity still eludes them—and men, they say, are to blame, adding that men are unhappy only because they haven't fully accepted the social paradigm of female equality and they need to break out of their old way of thinking and embrace this new feminized age. Traditional masculinity, the experts argue, keeps men from finding peace and fulfillment. They aren't emotional enough, connected to women enough, and hanging out in groups sharing their feelings enough. In other words, they're not feminine enough.

I agree with Moore and Gillette that the problem isn't men failing to embrace their inner feminine nature. It's that they're overwhelmed by the feminine. This problem is as real today as it was when they wrote their book in the early '90s. Attacks on masculinity are even worse now than they were then. At that time, the authors observed that men weren't connected to their masculinity in a way that led them into maturity because materialistic notions of what it meant to be a man were blocking them from developing into full manhood. Some of this could be blamed on fathers failing to initiate their sons into being men, but a large part of the blame is to be laid at the feet of a culture that has idolized the feminine. Women dominate in the home, schools, churches, and higher learning. The feminist agenda has greatly shaped the political landscape, as equality of outcomes is demanded through government intervention. Feminism has cast men adrift. "In this present crisis in masculinity we do not need, as some feminists are saying, less masculine power," Moore and Gillette write. "We need more. But we need more of the mature masculine."[9]

The purpose of my book is to help women get out of the feminist mindset of competing and seeking equality of outcomes with men and to focus on their relationships with men. Only through living according to our true purpose as men and women—and going on that journey together, supporting and helping each other—will we grow and mature into the loving people we were designed to be. That path isn't easy. It takes humility, sacrifice, and meekness to heal the rift between the sexes. Men have a part to play in that healing—it's not all on the women. If you're concerned about my heavy emphasis on women as the problem, turn to Chapter 8, where I address men's failures. But my primary purpose is not to focus on what men should do. There are countless books by feminists on the market doing just that. I consider my work "equal time." My goal is to talk to the ladies, to do as Katherine did and remind them of who men are, who they are designed to be, and how to love them so they can become great.

The soul of a man is a beautiful thing. Full of creativity, sensuality, connectivity, and passion. Men are curious about nature, feel enlivened when they're engaging with it, studying it, and unlocking its secrets. They adore women and love to serve us in a troubled world, save us from its dangers, bask in our beauty, sacrifice because they love us, and lift us up as queens ruling at their side. They feel deeply and put their hearts on the line. A man is not a woman's enemy. Though there are bad men in the world who hurt women in the most unimaginable ways, these are not the norm, nor should they define all men. Their evil presence is why women need good, strong men to protect them. Women need men to desire them, to care for them, to connect with them. It's how they're designed, and they're not complete without the other. Contrary to popular feminists' beliefs, women do need men—just like a fish needs water.

CHAPTER 2

# BELIEVE HIM

*In the name of God, do your duty. In the name of God, believe him.*

—Atticus Finch, Harper Lee's *To Kill a Mockingbird*

Nothing exemplifies better the silencing—and the frustrations—of men than the travesty of the confirmation hearings of Judge Brett Kavanaugh for the Supreme Court. They brought to light how men have been labeled as predators and left with little recourse to defend themselves. When I talk to men about what they'd like to say to women, one of the constant refrains is, "Don't condemn me just because I'm a man." During the hearings, we heard no such thing. Instead, we were inundated with demands to "believe her." I heard it repeatedly as Christine Blasey Ford testified before the Senate Judiciary Committee. She had accused Kavanaugh of sexual assault, and Democratic senators who didn't want him donning the SCOTUS black robe latched onto every word of Ford's conflicting testimony as proof that he was unfit.

An inquiry that should have been a matter of evidence and logical analysis transformed into an exercise of faith under the rubric of feminism and political game-play.

President Donald Trump's nomination had been controversial from the start. Kavanaugh is pro-life and a committed constitutional originalist. Democrats feared he would overturn *Roe v. Wade* and considered his addition to the court an attack on a woman's right to choose to abort her child—a sacrament in the religion of radical feminism. Ford's allegation was hope among the faithful that he would never see inside the Supreme Court.

Acting as if they'd be hauled into a man's bedroom like sex slaves if Kavanaugh were confirmed, protesters screamed outside—and sometimes inside—the Senate Office Building as the Judiciary Committee grilled him on his qualifications. After weathering the storm, the embattled judge faced another trial of a different sort—one that left him with little defense except for his word. He had to answer Ford's accusation that he had sexually assaulted her nearly forty years ago while they were in high school. He vehemently denied it but, like other political and legal figures before him, he faced a woman's charge that was enough to sink his hopes of ever fulfilling his dreams of public service—unless he somehow proved himself innocent.

## THE #METOO MOVEMENT TOOK A WRONG TURN IN ITS EXPOSURE OF SEXUAL PREDATORS.

Ford's salacious allegation came at a time when society's conscience had been pricked about the abuse of women in various industries, particularly in the media and Hollywood. While America has come far in its legal treatment of rape victims, bad men still exist, and abuse is present in the shadowed corners of CEO offices, movie sets, media parties, and many other settings that should be safe for women. The #MeToo movement, in which women banded together with their testimonies of rape and assault, exposed open secrets in professional circles. Scores of women came forth after actresses accused Hollywood power producer Harvey Weinstein of abuse. He was expelled from his position, later arrested, and charged with sexual assault, rape, and other offenses.

Led by professional women tired of being treated like meat in the movie business and feeling powerless, the #MeToo campaign aimed at weeding out predators from the industry and putting an end to the abuse of women in every sphere of life, from homes, to workplaces, to halls of power. In just a few months, the movement spread like wildfire across the globe as women came forth, telling their stories of sexual assault. I was one of those women, having suffered date rape in college, though I made a point of calling women to account in some (certainly not all) situations for their naïveté and, at times, lack of personal responsibility while dealing with naturally sexual creatures like the human male in common social circles. Feminists accused me of blaming the victim, but encouraging women to understand their own sexuality, to learn how to protect themselves preemptively, and to be wise in their interactions with men is hardly blaming the victim—it's one step in preventing future victims.

Like many movements that begin with the best intentions, #MeToo quickly devolved. Flirtation began to be cast as sexual harassment and even abuse. A stolen kiss on a date was interpreted as sexual assault. Vengeful women turned on former lovers by rewriting history and calling a consensual one-night stand rape. The ever-present reality of sexual tension between men and women—a fundamentally natural dynamic—became suspect as men were labeled potential predators ready to pounce. College students were some of the most heartbreaking targets as several were falsely accused, their reputations ruined, their relationships broken, and their aspirations shattered along with due process.

This treatment of men was hardly new; it had been a cornerstone of the overarching radical feminist narrative for decades, but it was intensifying. The #MeToo movement took a notably dark turn when women in the media produced a list of men who were accused of sexual abuse and harassment. No proof was given—only accusation, just a name on a list, put there by women who claimed to have been abused. Ghosts of Lenin's Red Terror in which the innocent were rounded up and declared guilty for mere association with a targeted group were rattling their chains in warning. Whether it leads to the horrific death of millions, jail time, or loss of employment, collective guilt is devastating to the individual, no matter the context. The #MeToo tactic had its intended effect, as media outlets threatened to fire any man whose name appeared on the list. Accusation became truth. Witch hunts ensued. President Donald Trump became a target of this line of attack, as women with unsubstantiated stories of rape crawled from cracks and crevices at critical political moments to try to defeat him where votes failed. Guilty until proven innocent became the standard of justice for men accused of the heinous crime of rape, sexual harassment, or sexual assault. Distrust seeped into relationships, cemented by group hostility and condemnation.

The corruption of the #MeToo movement also grew from the seeds of the tried-and-true political manipulations of leftist agitators seeking to overthrow those in power as part of the great Marxist struggle between the haves and the have-nots, the oppressors and the victims—a philosophy adopted by so-called progressives in America. The strategy of labeling enemies, freezing them in a moment in time with a hateful smear, and silencing them as society recoils from the stigma placed on them, was fully employed under the banner "Believe women."

## WOMEN WANT EQUALITY OF OUTCOMES, NOT EQUALITY.

#MeToo served as a rich opportunity to promote the notion that "the patriarchy" still rules over women, and men must be cast out from their positions of power—despite the glaring fact that women have already secured their rights in America's judicial system and are treated as equals in society. They're protected by anti-discrimination laws and ensured equal opportunity in employment, though not equal outcomes. More women are attending and graduating from college than men, and they dominate an education system that elevates and caters to girls, leaving boys to languish, confused about what it means to be masculine.

Women dominate more professions than ever, though they aren't the high-paying jobs feminists covet, despite women freely *choosing* to enter lower-paying professions. They include public relations managers, veterinarians, social and community managers, pharmacists, human resources managers, financial specialists, counselors, nurses, teachers, psychologists, tax preparers, insurance underwriters, advertising and promotions managers, among others. Yet women still claim to be oppressed, even though men overwhelmingly dominate the twenty most dangerous occupations in the United States. The fatality for men in the workplace is ten times that of women, but feminists aren't demanding equal representation in those jobs.[10] They want positions with status, big paychecks, and impressive titles. When it comes to equality in the job market, feminists are like single women who complain there aren't any worthy men to date because they only want to marry a rich guy.

No matter how free women have become, feminists demand more because the holy grail of equal outcomes has not been achieved. They strive and demand, but this equality eludes them because the fact remains—men and women aren't the same. Like socialists who make the rich poorer not the poor richer, they realize they can't hold all the same coveted positions of men due to differences in ability and choice, so they try another tactic: bringing men down. What better way to delegitimize a man and tear him from his pinnacle of success than to stamp him with the flaming brand of sexism in all its forms? Is it any accident that, in the wake of #MeToo, nearly all the men fired from their jobs due to sexual abuse allegations alone—whether credible or not—were replaced by women?

Despite its legitimate concerns, #MeToo went too far. It crossed a line, propelled by those who let fear and envy rob them of trust and fairness. Among the thousands of men broadly affected by the #MeToo movement, most never saw a trial, but they suffered anyway. They were cast as the villain in a drama written by and for feminists. Too many women had been taught by a culture saturated in propagandistic drivel from women's studies classes that men are a threat and women must always be believed. Feminists gung ho for the #MeToo movement and its focus on "believe her" to the detriment of due process propelled the movement away from seeking good for women to assuming bad in men. In response, men shut down and became suspicious, guarded, and angry that they were falsely accused, packed into a single group, and labeled sexist at best, rapist at worst. As feminists armed themselves in the red robes of *The Handmaid's Tale*—a fictional dystopia about women becoming sex slaves in the future—men looked around and wondered what the hell happened. How did they become anathema to social order, peace, and security? How did masculinity—once so prized in America—become toxic?

## MEN ARE INNOCENT UNTIL PROVEN GUILTY NO MATTER THE SETTING—LEGAL, PERSONAL, POLITICAL, OR PROFESSIONAL.

The hysteria of the #MeToo movement reached a climax in the Kavanaugh hearings as Ford weaved her story about him assaulting her at a party. Wide-eyed and speaking with a pitched baby voice to garner sympathy, she gave scant details about the incident, even failing to remember who took her home from the party after the life-altering attack. Shockingly, Democratic senators on the committee, who should have been seeking truth, prefaced their questioning of Ford with "We want you to know that we believe you." Without hearing one shred of testimony, they had already come to a verdict. In affirming Ford, they were saying, "We believe Kavanaugh is guilty."

As I sat at my desk that day, taking notes about the hearing and tweeting my thoughts, I grew angrier and angrier. I imagined my husband, my son, or my brother facing these accusations. The helplessness of being assumed guilty, of having the impossible task to prove one's innocence weighed on me. I've been in enough circumstances in my life in which I faced false accusations to feel the horror of it. It's a true injustice like no other. No credible corroborating evidence supported Ford's testimony. The words that came haltingly from her lips weren't plausible. Neither was her demeanor. Her lack of intense emotion betrayed her narrative. Her giggles and nonsensical distractions about being so afraid of people due to Kavanaugh's assault that she had to build extra doors in her house, despite admitting that she invited scores of students to her home, sent warning bells off in my head. I knew what it was like to be held down by a man stronger than me. I knew how dehumanizing it felt to be used as a tool for a man's release. Even after decades, I could still feel the anger burn inside of me. Ford's testimony rang hollow.

A case can be made, of course, that people respond to trauma differently. That's true, but I went with my gut on this. I simply didn't believe her claim that Kavanaugh was the man who assaulted her, and the burden of proof was on her and the system that was investigating the crime. From what I'd observed, there was no proof except this weak testimony brought against a man who had caused political upheaval because of his pro-life position and the possibility of putting abortion "rights" at risk if he were confirmed as a Supreme Court justice. The timing, the manner, the speciousness of her testimony supported my gut instinct.

So I tweeted about it. I said there's no credible evidence that Kavanaugh assaulted her. I believed something did happen to her, but I was not duty-bound as a fellow member of the female group to conclude that Kavanaugh had done it simply because she said so. I tweeted fervently as if talking to the television, which I might have done—"I don't believe you!" The response from men on Twitter was overwhelming. "Thank you for saying what we can't!" "Thank you for defending men!" Why couldn't they? They had been silenced, that's why. Because some individual men throughout history had raped and assaulted women, because women were actually abused and the justice system in the past looked the other way and even went so far as to blame the women, *all* men are now identified as the same—predators, whose traditional masculinity compels them to be sexual abusers.

## MEN ARE BEING STIGMATIZED INTO SILENCE ON THE BASIS OF COLLECTIVE GUILT.

Men have been effectively labeled as dangerous to women, and, as punishment and restitution, they must be stripped of their power in society. Men—especially straight white men—have been delegitimized, their words meaning little, an echo in a world screaming their guilt. The stigma stinks, and men know it. They feel it in their hearts. It affects their relationships. They endure the weight of prejudice as they sit in family court with "believe the mother" skewing many (though certainly not all) custody, alimony, and child support decisions. They experience it in the training sessions they endure at work to teach them how to be self-controlled little boys who know their place in the world. They're made to feel like a force to be eyed with suspicion, a class of humanity that has shone too brightly for too long. They're told they have held too much power throughout human history and need to be brought down so others can rise.

As pro-feminist Michael Kimmel writes in *Manhood in America*, men must develop a new egalitarian masculinity in which their primary calling is to secure equality of outcomes for all the groups in America that have been excluded from their "full humanity" by the exclusivity of men. The American male, Kimmel writes, must prove his manhood, his goodness for society, by lifting those kept down by traditional masculinity and joining the struggle of marginalized groups for their "rightful share of the sun."[11] He must put aside any historical or objective masculinity and live according to the principles of "democratic manhood." In other words, it's time for today's men to step aside and let women take their place, not because they earned it, but because women are part of a class that, in the past, had been oppressed by men. The individuality of men today doesn't matter; their respect for women's rights is ignored. They are part of a historical collective from which they can never excise themselves—at least, according to feminists who can't extract themselves from groupthink.

The day after Ford's testimony before the Senate Judicial Committee, Kavanaugh took the stand. His response was not what the feminists wanted or liked. He didn't just sit there and take it like the good little boy he was expected to be. His voice shook. He was angry. He cried. He became impassioned in the declaration of his innocence. He resorted to snark once in a while when he was pinned into a corner. In other words, he acted like any normal human on trial for something he didn't do, facing inquisitors who had already made up their minds. His entire life, reputation, career, family—all had been maligned because of a single, unsupported accusation of sexual assault from decades ago. Kavanaugh was fighting for his life.

The hearing reminded me of the trial in Harper Lee's *To Kill a Mockingbird* in which an African-American man was falsely accused of raping a white woman. He held his head up proudly and told the truth, his voice strained with fierce emotion, his eyes filled with nobility only the innocent possess. The mob was against him, whispering like snakes, "Believe her." He was presumed guilty. Only his lawyer, Atticus Finch, stood between him and a damning verdict.

"This case is not a difficult one," Finch said in his closing statement after witnesses clearly showed the man's innocence. It should never have come to trial, he continued. The state didn't produce any evidence that the crime even took place. Instead, they relied on "the testimony of two witnesses whose evidence has not only been called into serious question on cross-examination but has been flatly contradicted by the defendant."[12] In Kavanaugh's case, there was only one witness—Ford—and she couldn't even remember how she got home after the supposed attack.

The prejudice in *To Kill a Mockingbird* was against black people. The prejudice in Kavanaugh's hearing was against men. It wasn't in a courtroom that this bigotry was exposed, but in the court of public opinion and in a political sphere that can ruin lives as thoroughly as any trial before a judge and jury. The same words Finch used about assuming the guilt of blacks could be said about assuming the guilt of men today. He called that assumption evil, and that's exactly what it is. It's the belief that all men deceive, that all men are basically immoral beings, and that all men are not to be trusted around women. These assumptions are lies, he said. The truth is that *some* men lie, *some* men are immoral, *some* men are abusers. This truth, however, applies to the entire human race and not to one particular sex. Some women lie, some women are immoral, some women are abusers.

"There is not one person in this courtroom who has never told a lie," Finch said, "who has never done an immoral thing, and there is no man living who has never looked upon a woman without desire."[13] He then launched into a speech that, though fictional, is no less true and fits perfectly into the frame of #MeToo, feminism, equality of outcomes, and loss of due process.

> Thomas Jefferson once said that all men are created equal.... There is a tendency...for certain people to use this phrase out of context, to satisfy all conditions [equality of outcomes]. The most ridiculous example I can think of is that people who run public education promote the stupid and idle along with the industrious—because all men are created equal, educators will gravely tell you, the children left behind suffer terrible feelings of inferiority. We know all men are not created equal in the sense some people would have us believe—some people are smarter than others, some people have more opportunity because they're born with it, some men make more money than others, some ladies make better cake than others—some people are born gifted beyond the normal scope of men. But there is one way in this country which all men are created equal—there is one human institution that makes a pauper the equal of a Rockefeller, the

> stupid man equal of an Einstein, and an ignorant man equal of any college president. That institution, gentlemen, is a court. It can be the Supreme Court of the United States or the humblest J.P. court in the land, or this honorable court which you serve. Our courts have their faults, as does any human constitution, but in this country our courts are the great levelers, and in our courts all men are created equal.[14]

Heavy with the weight of responsibility, Finch ended with a powerful statement: "In the name of God, do your duty. In the name of God, believe him."

Such words are heresy today. We are told to believe the accuser, not the accused—that's the essence of the #MeToo message. Yet, when it comes to our legal system, the court of public opinion, politics, the workplace, and even hearings for the nomination of a Supreme Court justice, we should believe not the accuser with no credible evidence, but the accused who is unable to establish his innocence, who could never prove a negative. It is our duty and responsibility to hold onto this foundational principle of liberty as tightly as a rope tossed to a drowning man. It is how we show mutual affection and—dare I say—love to one another. It's beyond power dynamics. It's beyond righting historical wrongs. It's beyond equality of outcomes. It's far beyond demanding a place in the sun. It's respecting the equal treatment of all humans crafted in the image of God. It's fundamentally about freedom.

CHAPTER 3

# MEN—YES, WE NEED THEM

*We make men without chests and expect of them virtue and enterprise. We laugh at honor and are shocked to find traitors in our midst. We castrate and bid the geldings be fruitful.*

—C. S. Lewis

"Stop treating me as if I'm irrelevant!" I can't tell you how many times I've heard this repeated by men when asked what they'd like to say to women but can't. You might be tempted to think they're overreacting, but they have a good reason to feel this way. In 2012, Greg Hampikian wrote an article in *The New York Times* titled "Men, Who Needs Them?" in which he describes how men are becoming irrelevant in both reproduction and parenting. "Women aren't just becoming men's equals," Hampikian writes. "It's increasingly clear that 'mankind' itself is a gross misnomer: an uninterrupted, intimate and essential maternal connection defines our species.... With expanding reproductive choices, we can expect to see more women choose to reproduce without men entirely."[15] Of course, women will still need men to donate sperm, but women are increasingly choosing to raise children without fathers. Hampikian was curious to know whether feminists thought anything about men was irreplaceable, so he asked a female colleague what she thought. "They're entertaining," she quipped in response. Such women who utter such disrespect for their counterparts in a world designed for them to work together deserve Katherine's moniker: "weak, ungovernable worms." Hampikian ended his article with an attitude of defeat: "Gentlemen, let's hope that's enough."[16] I can guarantee it's not. For one thing, a selfish woman will always find other forms of entertainment. But, more importantly, when a man has been deemed irrelevant and his very nature is disrespected, the last thing he will be is entertaining.

## IF "THE FUTURE IS FEMALE," THEN WE'RE IN FOR ONE HELL OF A NASTY RIDE.

In 2013, *New York Times* columnist Maureen Dowd joined three other feminists at an organized debate in Canada to discuss the question, "Are men obsolete?" The very question spoke volumes about a not-so-subversive feminist agenda to delegitimize men and pave the way for a future dominated by women—a goal immortalized in the campaign "The Future is Female." This call for female empowerment made its debut in 1975 on a T-shirt sold in a New York feminist bookstore as part of the lesbian separatist movement. Celebrities revived it in 2015 as Trump plowed his way toward the White House, and in 2017—after her humiliating loss to the political outsider—Hillary Clinton echoed the slogan in an attempt to rally the troops. This dismissal of men was the same attitude reflected in the debate when Dowd said without reservation, "Men are so last century. They seem to have stopped evolving, sulking like Achilles in his tent. The mahogany-paneled, McClelland's scotch and rum and 'Mad Men' world is disappearing…as they struggle to figure out the altered parameters of manliness and resist becoming house-dudes."[17]

One of the more disturbing observations about the feminist agenda is found in the book *Professing Feminism: Cautionary Tales from Inside the Strange World of Women's Studies* by Daphne Patai and Noretta Koertge in which they compare modern feminism to a religious cult with its unrelenting dogma, demand for conformity of thought, and hostility to those they see as threats—namely, men. Feminism, they write, is no longer about equal rights for women.

> It aspires to be much more than this. It bids to be a totalizing scheme resting on a grand theory, one that is all-inclusive as Marxism, as assured of its ability to unmask hidden meanings as Freudian psychology, and as fervent in its condemnation of apostates as evangelical fundamentalism. Feminist theory provides a doctrine of original sin: the world's evils originate in male supremacy. It regards the male's (usually: the white male's) insistence on maintaining his own power as the passkey that unlocks the mysteries of individual actions and institutional behavior. And it offers a prescription for radical change that is as simple as it is drastic: reject whatever is tainted with patriarchy and replace it with something embodying gynecentric [sic] values.[18]

Modern feminism has taken an even more hostile turn against men with the rise of intersectional feminism, the sociological theory spawned in the bowels of academia that focuses on how women's overlapping identities (sexual orientation, gender identity, race, religion, physical disabilities—the list can really go on forever) determine how they've experienced oppression and discrimination. A person's various identities affect how much of a victim she is and how justified she is in making sure the "privileged" in society right all wrongs against her. A gay black woman, for example, would be considered more oppressed and therefore deserving greater social justice than a straight white woman. It's not clear whether a Muslim woman or a disabled black woman trumps the gay black woman. Maybe if the disabled black woman also had a peanut allergy or female baldness, she'd be on top of the oppressed pyramid. The order of victimization is not always apparent because our intersectional identities are as varied as the number of people on the planet.

One thing, however, is crystal clear: According to intersectional theory, the least oppressed, most "privileged," and, therefore, the biggest target of social justice, is the Christian straight white man. Lawyer and academic Alan Dershowitz disagrees that Christians are the main focus, making the case that intersectionality is more anti-Semitic than anti-Christian, calling it a "code word for anti-American, anti-Western, anti-Israel and anti-Semitic bigotry." He cites intersectional propaganda with the haunting refrain: "ending white privilege starts with ending Jewish privilege."[19] This attitude has certainly been reflected in recent women's marches in which intersectional feminists have claimed that they are natural allies of anti-Israel Muslims.

Philosopher and author of *The War Against Boys: How Misguided Policies are Harming Our Young Men*, Christina Hoff Sommers says intersectional feminism has hijacked classical equity feminism, which focuses on freedoms for women, not equality of outcomes.

This new breed of feminists "demand trigger warnings, safe spaces, and micro-aggression monitoring. Their primary focus is not equality with men—but rather protection from them."[20] Ironically, these empowered feminists treat women as if they're fragile and the advances made by our mothers and grandmothers for equal rights didn't amount to much. Men, they believe, still function as a privileged group that keeps women down, but, as Sommers points out, this is hardly the case.

> Girls and women are the privileged sex in education. From preschool to graduate school, and across ethnic and class lines, women get better grades, they win most of the honors and prizes, and they're far more likely to go to college. Today women earn a majority of bachelor's degrees and advanced degrees. Latino girls are now slightly more likely to attend college than white boys. When an education policy analyst looked at current trends in higher education he quipped, only half in jest, "The last male will graduate from college in 2068." [citation omitted] Our schools have offered untold number of admirable and effective programs to strengthen girls in areas where they languished—in sports, math, and science. Where are the programs to help boys in areas where they falter: reading, writing, grades, school engagement and college matriculation? So far Congress, schools of education, school boards and the Department of Education have looked the other way.[21]

## FEMINISM IS THE REAL TOXICITY IN TODAY'S CULTURE—AND IT GENERATES FEAR AMONG WOMEN.

Despite these facts, modern feminists still think men are privileged and that women need to be protected from them. What is at the root of this fear? Some say the problem lies with men—they haven't learned to be nice enough or show the proper amount of empathy because they're still driven by hostile, toxic masculinity. But this isn't the problem at all. While first-wave feminists who sought more freedom for women focused on individual rights, they weren't afraid of men. We didn't hear most of them decrying male masculinity. Most of the first feminists wanted equality for the betterment of the family and their relationships with men. It was only later that motherhood, family, fathers, and husbands became stigmatized in the feminist lexicon. Feminism went awry when it sought equity instead of equality, and when women stopped wanting to be free to be the best women they could be as individuals, mothers, wives, friends, and American citizens and started wanting to be like men. Feminism has strayed from its former mission and has embraced an agenda "to promote women's full autonomy by eliminating gender distinctions and forcing gender parity (statistical proportionality of males and females) in every area of academic, economic, social, and political life," Christina Villegas of The Heritage Foundation accurately writes in "The Modern Feminist Rejection of Government."[22]

This desire for sameness ignited deep anxiety in the feminist soul, and it's a fear that will never go away as long as the goal is equity—not because a man's masculinity is toxic, but because women have set themselves up for failure with the aim of equal outcomes. They want to be on equal footing with men regarding their very identity. While they assert that they don't believe men and women are the "same," their demand for equal outcomes and desire to transform masculinity into a tame form of femininity belies their claim. They want to establish a state of existence in which there is no tension, no competition, and no natural conflicts. Women want a peaceful coexistence in which men dutifully step aside and let women shine in the sun and do whatever they want to do.

This utopia will never happen because women will never have the kind of equality of conditions they desire. Even if every man were socially compliant, women who have set themselves in opposition to men would still feel like they need protection because men will continue to be, at the very least, physically stronger than women. This natural inequality creates an ever-present fear of men among women. It generates profound insecurity, which is the feminist conundrum. In their quest for equity, they put themselves in perpetual conflict with men, not merely because they are competing with them—which equality of opportunity fosters—but because they are losing the competition, or at least not winning as often or in the way women would like.

As soon as women gained their equal rights—and rightly so—they turned their eyes toward a different kind of equality, the kind that disrupts relationships, undermines society, and destroys freedom. Equality in the classical sense wasn't enough; they wanted all the privileges and successes men had achieved. But to reach that height, they had to compete. As a result, some women succeeded; some women didn't. That would have been satisfactory if the goal had been solely to participate in society without obstacles being placed in their way—social barriers denying them opportunity. But it wasn't. They wanted the holy grail of equity—a prize they'll never win. The problem is that competition, which is born of equal rights, doesn't bring equality of outcomes. Quite the contrary. It reveals even more inequality, and the most pervasive inequalities between men and women are physical strength and innate differences based on a woman's maternal design, which adds to her vulnerability. Male strength is accompanied by other traits that set men apart from women, but male power alone is enough to fuel fear in women.

If men and women don't trust one another, the tension of a man's strength and a woman's physical weakness, especially regarding sexual vulnerability, will be exacerbated. I believe this is one of the core insecurities underpinning the modern feminist movement. Fueled by their desire for equity, women have separated themselves from the comfort of a man's strength and positioned themselves in opposition to it. But in this battle, they cannot win. This realization—whether they acknowledge it or not—drives them to belittle men, bring them down to their level, and manipulate men into transforming into nonthreatening nice guys who are vulnerable and need to share their feelings in groups. It also compels women to continually seek government intervention to level the playing field. It creates a culture of male guilt in which men feel ashamed of their strength because they're told it's toxic, so they go to group therapy to share their emotions, take medications to stifle their aggression, and join fathers' clubs in which they carry their babies in papooses and dance in groups.

Feminist Betty Friedan once said that women live a life of quiet desperation. The Women's Liberation Movement supposedly freed them from that. But it didn't. Those who seek equity still live in quiet desperation because they are constantly afraid of men. They've gained equality, but they're still unsettled, anxious, and fearful. No matter how much men say they respect women and their rights, feminists today don't trust them because a man's masculine nature is a threat to women—the inequality of conditions between them puts women in a fearful position no matter the motives or intents of men.

As a result, men are cast as the enemy, told they're irrelevant, or pressured into changing their powerful masculinity into benign and safe democratic manhood. The strategy today is that if women can't achieve equality of conditions with men, then men must change. We see this most clearly in the new American Psychological Association Guidelines for Psychological Practice with Boys and Men in which "traditional masculinity" is recast as sexually abusive, emotionally stoic, and overly aggressive.[23] The APA assumes that masculinity is mostly a social construct, so society can change it to meet its current needs and agendas. The main goal of our culture today is equity, so men are told they must be more vulnerable, emotionally connected, gentle, sexually submissive, and open about their feelings. In other words, they need to stop being the bulwark of strength that built civilization. Stop being strong in a way that makes women feel threatened. Stop being sexually drawn to women in a way that makes them feel uncomfortable. Stop being men.

According to Ronald Levant, former APA president and one of the main researchers who influenced the new APA guidelines, men are in crisis today because they can't handle the changes feminism has brought to the male-female relationship. He says that for men to be happy, they need to stop avoiding their own femininity; restricting their emotions; being sexually disconnected and homophobic, pursuing achievement and status; relying on themselves; and believing that strength, courage, and aggression are the most valuable of manly virtues. "The bottom line is that men possess a host of admirable skills and traits," Levant writes, "but emotional intelligence isn't one of them."[24]

The problem with Levant's conclusions is that he has fallen for confirmation bias. He assumes that men are depressed and struggling today because their masculinity can't adjust to the new world order dictated by feminism. He concludes that men must change. While the adjustment to women's equality has been a factor in the lives of modern men, they have generally done a great job accommodating changes. Men support women working, help in the home, and encourage women to participate in all aspects of society with general ease. The problem isn't men unable to deal with the equality of women. It's men unable to be themselves because of feminism's quest for equity. The cause of their angst isn't false masculinity, but an inability to live out their purpose as men in a society that maligns masculinity and seeks to reconstruct it—hence the title of Levant's book, *Masculinity Reconstructed: Changing the Rules of Manhood—At Work, in Relationships, and in Family Life.*

In a society in which men are told that they are irrelevant, where boys have little guidance into manhood, and where women are increasingly dismissive of masculine traits and purposes, men are experiencing their own quiet desperation. The answer isn't to reconstruct their masculinity but to help them find meaning as men in the world today. This act of love for a fellow human being requires women to understand who a man is, what his purpose is as an individual and in relationship to the feminine, and how to help him live according to his nature and to fulfill his destiny and responsibilities as a man. Women need to fall in love with men again, not erotically but reverently with *agape* love—the highest form of love that originates from God and extends to our fellow human beings. It is a profoundly respectful love based on a deep value of another person's worth. This is the love women need to rekindle for men in our society as they embrace sexual differences, value others because they are made in the image of God, and celebrate masculinity as much as they celebrate femininity.

## REAL MEN AREN'T GOING TO SIT BY AND JUST TAKE IT—INSTEAD, THEY'LL GO THEIR OWN WAY TO THE DETRIMENT OF EVERYONE.

One of the lessons of modern feminists is that women don't need men. So for decades, women have been going their own way while still demanding all the perks and benefits of men in the home, in the workplace, and in society. Women freely abandon their homes while men are left picking up the tab. Women demand equal pay, but not for equal work. Women insist on equal representation in various professions but leave all the uncelebrated tough jobs to men. Women get the benefit of the doubt in domestic abuse cases, even though they are also violent and guilty of killing more young children in the home than men. As reported by NBC News, "Experts say more mothers than fathers kill their children under 5 years of age. And some say our reluctance as a society to believe mothers would be capable of killing their offspring is hindering our ability to recognize warning signs, intervene and prevent more tragedies." According to Cheryl Meyer, co-author of *Mothers Who Kill their Children*, "A mother kills a child in this country once every three days, and that's a low estimate."[25]

And this number doesn't even include voluntary abortions. All of this while masculinity has been attacked over and over again, deemed toxic, and labeled abusive.

Did feminists think men would sit by and take it, curl into a little ball, and whimper, "Hit me again"? Of course not. Men in America have responded to modern feminism and its oppression of the masculine in three ways. Some men have become compliant, bowing to the will of the feminists and handing over their masculinity in exchange for some measure of peace (and sex). No doubt, these are some of the men in Levant's studies who saw "improvement" in their relationships when they started acting more like women. Most men look for ways to function in the chaos and confusion, holding onto some measure of sanity but suffering the effects of the assault against them. These men are inwardly angry, frustrated, and somewhat bitter, but they don't want to abandon their relationships with women. They love women, but they don't want to sacrifice their manhood at the altar of feminism.

Other men have bowed out completely. They've receded into what the internet calls the "manosphere," in which they seek their dreams separate from marriage to women. Men Going Their Own Way (MGTOW) is one group that represents these men who have given up on women, mainly in romantic relationships, and refuse to give in to the feminist agenda. While these men are not the majority, they are a significant group when it comes to seeing what modern feminism has created. By saying men are irrelevant, feminists have created a reactionary group that says women are irrelevant—at least in marriage. Most Americans are somewhere in the middle of these two groups, but it would be unwise not to consider them—for the radicals of today that have little impact on public policy often become the dictators of norms tomorrow.

As feminism has driven a wedge between men and women, these men who are tired of it no longer want a relationship with a woman. They want self-ownership. Instead of living to provide for and protect women, which is part of their designed purpose as men, they seek to guard their sovereignty and property above everything else; individuality and independence reign supreme. Sound familiar? They're an echo of the feminists of today. As MGTOW says on its website, men choosing to distance themselves from women "is the manifestation of one word: 'No.'" They refuse to be defined and controlled by the experts who say that their masculinity must be reconstructed. They no longer want to live as women tell them to live, to be the nice guy, the good guy, and the doormat for women who think they can be everything a man is and use them to try to reach that delusion. MGTOW says they've had enough, and they refuse "to bow, serve and kneel for the opportunity to be treated like a disposable utility." Instead, they want to live according to their own best interests "in a world which would rather [men] didn't."[26]

These men argue that "if MGTOW is fire, then perhaps feminism is gasoline," and "every action has an equal and opposite reaction."[27] So, like the feminists, they go their own way, saying a man needs a woman like a fish needs a bicycle, echoing the famous feminist mantra to the contrary. These men would rather live as monks than deal with feminists. It's hard not to blame them for this attitude, but the bitterness runs deep, as it has with the feminists. "Survival and mating are the success model for animals in the wild," these men say. "That's the best they will ever do. But marriage and children are not the highest pinnacles of success for men. Some 60 percent of men who ever lived on Earth never had children, so what did they dedicate their lives to? For millennia, men have accomplished and contributed far greater miracles of science, discovery and human endeavor."[28]

Men have accomplished great things, and most of us want them to go on achieving a great deal more, not to the exclusion of women, but to seek dominion over a wild and sometimes hostile world for the sake of women they love. Where MGTOW goes wrong is they think this *must* happen without being in a relationship with women, or even doing it for women and the family. They cite inventors and explorers who achieved great things supposedly because they weren't married. Wilbur Wright's quote, "I don't have time for a wife and an airplane" is prominent in the MGTOW lexicon.

The idea that men can't and shouldn't seek greatness if they're married to a woman is untrue, of course. Bach was married. Most all of the founding fathers were married, including John Adams to a woman who serves as a shining example of how to be strong in herself yet a faithful helpmate to her husband. Thomas Edison was married twice, and his second wife Mina was a powerhouse all her own. She ran a grand estate, raised his children from his first marriage, and helped Edison in his business affairs. She handled all his public relationships so he could be busy doing what he loved: inventing. Mina fiercely guarded Edison's privacy so his mind could be free to discover. As she cared for his home, his children, and tended to his business, she also became a horticulturalist and worked tirelessly in the community for educational and religious causes to benefit those who lived around them. She was a woman of profound learning, always studying and keeping her husband engaged with enlivening conversation.

The marriage between Edison and Mina was a creative partnership in which both reached greatness. It is a prime example of mature masculinity and mature femininity in marriage. They had mutual respect, a shared destiny, and love for each other. Historians say that had she not provided such a stable and nurturing environment for Edison to work, we probably wouldn't benefit from his inventions today.

My point is that both modern feminists and the MGTOW movement are wrong in their reactions to social ills. Neither fosters relationships. Neither promotes love or unity. Neither respects the purpose of the masculine and feminine to work in concert to create, develop, raise families, progress, and spread *agape* love throughout the earth. Like the reactionary feminists, these men seek separation, not healing. They want to live their own lives, not sacrifice their lives for wives and children. They want to move mountains to create their own paths, and they want to do it alone. This is not mature masculinity. This is masculinity that has been deeply wounded by immature, selfish women. When a person is hurting, they are angry, they recoil into themselves and strike out when they feel threatened, and they see everyone who isn't 100 percent for them as the enemy.

The last thing I would say to these men is to "man up" in dealing with this feminist culture. I've done this in the past, and I realize it's like throwing salt into a gaping wound. Men have heard enough about manning up. They recognize what a man's calling should be in relation to women. They understand that a man is happy when he protects and cares for his family, when he "goes forth and conquers, gives of himself for a greater cause."[29] They are just tired of being dumped on and, in a way—who can blame them?

The answer, however, isn't to check out. If women or men continue to be alone, they will never find healing. What we need most in our society is not more individualism in a nihilistic sense, but more unity as men and women live together as complements, not as distant adversaries. To do this, women need to understand the pain they've inflicted, the wounds they have caused to fester, and the role they've played in creating their own misery. Mostly, they need to gain a new understanding and appreciation for men. They need to empathize with the male identity—not as defined by a woman, but as designed by God—to be providers, leaders, protectors, and procreators. Or, to put these in Jungian archetypical terms, the universal patterns of collective male unconsciousness: magicians, kings, warriors, and lovers.

CHAPTER 4

# MEN AS MAGICIANS (WOMEN ARE SO BITCHY)

*The human magician is always an initiate himself, and one of his tasks is to initiate others. But of what does he initiate? The Magician is an initiate of secret and hidden knowledge of all kinds.*

—Robert Moore and Douglas Gillette

"Women are my most difficult employees," my boss uttered with exasperation. His boldness in sharing such a thought with me in the days of feminism was startling, but he knew I would understand and not take offense. He'd heard me express the same frustration numerous times, so we were both in a safety zone. I also respected that he was including me in the mix of "most difficult employees"—it was a fact I couldn't very well deny. Generally speaking—and especially compared to men—women in the workplace are difficult. They're backstabbing, emotional, whiney, bitter, and nastily competitive.

Samantha Brick, a television executive producer of top shows on networks such as MTV, found out the truth of this when she started a female-only company, thinking it would be a utopia after working in the male-dominated television industry. Her business eventually failed because of the infighting among the all-girls staff, leaving her with a new understanding that women never really graduate from high school. "It was an idealistic vision swiftly shattered by the nightmare reality," Brick writes at the *UK Daily Mail*. "Constant bitchiness, surging hormones, unchecked emotion, attention-seeking and fashion rivalry so fierce it tore my staff apart. When I read the other day that Sienna Miller had said that there is no such thing as 'the Sisterhood,' I knew what she meant."[30]

Just after hiring seven women to start her new business, Brick noticed that two cliques quickly developed: "Those who had worked together before and those who were producing 'new ideas.'"[31] During coffee breaks and lunch, some were invited while others were excluded. The women gossiped about the fashion choices of other employees. "The office was like a Milan catwalk, but with the competitiveness of a Miss World contest—and the low cunning of a mud-wrestling bout," Brick writes. "It didn't take long for the office to become divided between the girls who wore make-up and those who didn't. Comments from the former were typically 'Doesn't she know what spot cover-up is?' or 'Has she ever met a hairbrush?' while the no-make-up clan were equally biting, with comments—behind their backs, naturally—such as 'People on the morning bus must think she's a prostitute'; or 'She looks like a slapper.'"[32]

Yikes, I can relate. Women are vicious—especially when they're passive-aggressive, slithering through the office like snakes in the grass, undermining everyone they can't compete with face-to-face. They're cowardly manipulators who play the actress to get what they want, and Brick saw this time and again in her office space of female bitchiness.

> Many of the women were aggressive or defensive, or both. The most aggressive masked a host of insecurities with their outgoing nature, while the defensive ones opened up only when provoked. The worst type I encountered, however, was the "passive aggressive"—She doesn't seem mean, but is the worst of the pack, ruthlessly bringing you down in such a sweet and unassuming manner that you don't realise what she's done until long after the event. She conceals her bitchy words in flowery phrases—one of my staff told another sweetly: "I don't mean to be a bitch, but I just can't bear to be in the same room and breathe the same air as you right now."[33]

Wow, this could describe my own experiences working with women in the media. It's a brutal warzone marked with lipstick kisses. I know what some of you might be thinking: "But I have a great female boss!" "I love the ladies I work with. They're awesome." "The men in my workplace are the intolerable ones." As with everything in this book, I'm using generalities. They're fair generalities, but they are generalities nonetheless. There are always exceptions, and workplaces vary in how people interact. I'm a woman and, if I'm going to generalize about women, I need to include myself, and I do it freely. I'm both guilty of being difficult and self-aware enough to be honest about it and seek change. This isn't the case with all women. They refuse to confirm the experiences of many people that women in the workplace are at least more stressful to deal with than men. This reality—along with additional complaints by women about "equal pay"—has created tension between men and women, and it needs to be addressed if we're going to learn to appreciate men in their role as providers.

After convincing several men to trust me with their thoughts about women in the professional arena, they had some pretty brutal things to say:

"Women get emotional and take everything so damn personally. The only exception is beta males who have been trained to act like women by women."

"Women need to stop trying to puff themselves up all the time, trying to be something they're not. They just need to relax and do the work."

"My female employees are often a pain in the ass. The men get along fine. If they disagree with you, they get over it. The women sulk, complain, and won't let you forget that they're unhappy about how you're managing the office."

"These women who have achieved so much need to grow the hell up. That's it. Stop acting like princesses."

"Neither society nor men owe women anything. This needs to be said in a generation where entitlement has reached an all-time high. Companies do not have to hire you because you're a woman nor are you owed any respect that you don't give. You aren't exempt from criticism."

"Women need to quit bitching about not being allowed at the adult table with the men and then when the heat comes your way once there, you cry your feminist bullshit. The fact that you're getting the heat along with the men means you've arrived in equality."

"Women need to quit using their sexuality to try and get men to do their work for them. They want equal pay? Do your own damn work!"

"Male professionals call each other out all the time. I don't think it is possible to call out stupid or incompetent women who are, frankly, stupid or incompetent, because that's deemed misogynist. I know tons of women professionals who are way past their skill level."

## EQUALITY DOESN'T GUARANTEE SUCCESS.

So what's up with women in the workplace, and why do they drive men (and each other) crazy? Why do they complain as if they're somehow disadvantaged? More women go to college than men. More women are hired than men when they graduate. Opportunities for women are at an all-time high. I know feminists say, "More needs to be done," but they measure this claim with manipulated numbers based on the goal of social uniformity with men instead of considering what women really want. Feminists determine equality by gender parity (equal numbers of men and women in politics, academia, and the workplace) and whether they're making the same amount overall. This equality of outcomes—similar to guaranteeing that everyone makes the same score on a test—is the goal of feminism today and undermines the differences between men and women and the nature of individuality.

According to Christina Villegas of The Heritage Foundation, this goal of modern feminism would require a transformation of American society and the Constitution with its protections of individual rights: "Achieving these ends requires the vast expansion of centralized government, the redefinition of freedom, and the preferential application of the law to women based on their identity as a specially protected class."[34] She continues:

> Building on the liberal feminist view that women can achieve self-actualization only by pursuing creative work outside of the home and the more radical belief that, aside from anatomy, there are essentially no innate differences between men and women, contemporary feminists presume that if women are truly free and equal, they will pursue the same goals as men. The dilemma for contemporary feminists is that although American women have gradually overcome the formal legal and informal cultural barriers that previously prevented them from participating in certain occupations and professions, this achievement has not led to statistical parity between the sexes in all areas of social, economic, and political life.[35]

Since feminists don't believe there are any differences between men and women beyond anatomy, they assume that any disparity in the workplace, or "social inequality," is due to discrimination. They extend this assumption to hiring practices and disparity in pay. You've probably seen the figure that women make about seventy-two to seventy-nine cents to every dollar a man earns. If you look at this alone, you'd think there is unfair pay disparity and that women are getting paid less for doing equal work.

This isn't the case. These numbers include the total of what all women make compared to the amount all men earn. It's not a comparison of specific jobs in which equality can truly be measured. Not all women want to work. Not all women want to go into science, technology, engineering, and math professions. Not all women have the same skill level as men. Not all women negotiate the same contracts as men (only to regret it later and then blame everyone else except themselves for making a bad deal). These differences are the devils in the details.

When it comes to having equal representation in all professions, feminists aren't honest about what they want. Because they assume men and women are the same and outcomes would be equal if only men weren't so sexist, they can't be honest about the innate differences between the sexes and the choices women make based on those differences. For example, they don't want to do the dangerous jobs men do—even the feminists avoid citing those jobs when they talk about equality. Their eye is on the professions that pay the big bucks or have status—the CEOs, political leaders, doctors, and military officers. We don't hear a lot about loggers, fishers, roofers, trash collectors, iron and steel workers, truck drivers, and construction workers. "Why aren't more women dying in their professions just like the men?" is not something you'll hear a feminist utter. Interestingly, we don't hear most men complaining about it either. That's because they're men, and they accept danger as part of the job.

## The demand for equal pay is a trap.

Women are guaranteed by America's anti-discrimination laws to get equal pay for equal work—this is the legal equality traditional feminists achieved. Some people try to violate those laws, but that's why we have laws. We have laws against stealing because there are bank robbers in the world. We're not going to rid society of bank robbers any more than we're going to be free of sexists and bigots. Some employers are going to try to discriminate based on skin color, religion, and sex. It happens all the time. Just go down to your local courthouse and read the complaints that are filed daily. I used to be a news reporter covering civil cases—people often try to discriminate just as they often see discrimination where there isn't any. These cases aren't easy to prove, but the law can only do so much. Any other form of force to impose social equality would violate liberty. The best we can do is establish and enforce anti-discrimination laws—and we have, albeit imperfectly. If a woman is doing the same job as a man, with the same qualifications brought to that job, and working the same hours, then she should be paid the same as the man. If she's not, she has a juicy lawsuit on her hands.

But here's the thing. Feminists aren't complaining about this very narrow understanding of equal pay. They've broadened it, expecting women to get the same pay as men—no matter the inequality of work. Never mind that the woman doesn't have the same work history because she left her career in the past to have children. Never mind that the woman hasn't put in the same hours as the man. Never mind that she's not as skilled as the man and that she doesn't generate the same revenue to form a basis of equal pay—a reality we see in male and female sports. These natural distinctions and liberties of women, which skew their job choices and subsequent pay, are ignored by feminists who demand "equal pay." They run back to that "wage gap" statistic as proof of discrimination. It isn't. This general number is not unequal pay for equal work. It is a wage gap created by natural differences and a woman's freedom.

Women choose to go into low-paying fields because they're more flexible. This freedom allows them to have time to raise their children. Women aren't as interested in STEM as feminists want them to be. Even if they graduate with a STEM degree, they don't always remain in the field because they have other interests. Many women don't want to be in the military, in the police force, or in any other profession that puts their lives at risk. They prefer to leave that to men, and they're grateful for it—or they should be. More men want to be politicians than women. More men want to take on the high-intensity (bordering on the insane) job of CEO at high-profile companies—a fact that riles feminists who want to see more women in these positions despite women opting for jobs with less pressure.

## Women have a problem with male competition.

Women have achieved a lot professionally, and a *qualified* woman can be considered for any job in America. Nothing stands in her way except for her own choices, qualifications, and ability to compete with others. The early feminists opened the door for women to enter a wide range of professions dominated by men—and entering the "world of men" is a *competitive* endeavor. Getting a job needs to be earned. Employers aren't running charity operations. Women have to contend with others to get into school, beat fellow job candidates, and outperform coworkers. The door that feminism opened for women was an opportunity to vie for advancement, and it is one that many women, including me, have benefited from greatly. I wouldn't be writing this book if it weren't for traditional feminists who knocked down barriers for women to compete in many areas of society outside the domestic sphere. But this newfound opportunity to compete is one of the main reasons women are so difficult in the workplace.

After women entered the arena of competition, many feminists still had the notion of equality ringing in their ears. It wasn't enough to be equal to men by removing barriers to opportunity. Feminists began to measure equality not according to rights and opportunities, but according to numbers. How many women are in a given profession—is that number equal to men? How much are women paid—is it equal to men? How many women succeed in competition? Is it equal to men? Equality moved from equality in freedom to equality of outcomes. This changed everything for women (and men)—and not for the better.

The problem is that when you compete, you might lose. Women have succeeded in many areas in their competition with men, but they have also failed. Some because they stopped trying and wanted to move on to something else—like having children. Others because they simply weren't good enough. As many strides as women have made, they are still not equal in outcome to men. Men still dominate in many areas. Men still fill the ranks of many professions, such as those dangerous jobs we discussed. Men still lead in technology and the sciences. Even some creative fields, such as the culinary arts, are still dominated by men—though women have made their strides, and the most decorated chef in the world at this time is a woman. Clearly, women have achieved great success—just watch any women's march and they'll be sure to give you the list of female accomplishments as they talk about the power of the woman and how the future is female.

But they're still not satisfied, because equity—equality of outcomes—has not been achieved. This frustration creates tension within the professional environment in which women are driven to succeed. When they can't, they don't look in the mirror and see themselves as the cause due to inabilities or choices by women who don't walk in lock step with the feminist cause. Instead, they focus their ire on society and blame others for impeding their progress. They assume men, always seen as the privileged class, are keeping women in a state of inequality.

This hunger for equity, along with an insufferable attitude of entitlement and unwillingness to face the consequences of competition, creates a discontented atmosphere in which women eye men with suspicion. Instead of women competing on merit, they demand privileges and benefits (which they call "rights") instead of working according to their abilities. Managers are pressured to hire employees not on their merit but on their sexuality and race—all in the name of diversity instead of quality. This attitude creates a divide between men and women, as men resent how feminism has created an unfair playing field: men still have to achieve through merit, but women get a break in the name of equality. Hence, the comment by one man who said, "If you can't compete, go home!"

The quest for equity has severed trust within the workplace. If competition were based solely on merit, everyone would shake hands at the end of the day and be happy. The best man—or woman—wins. But, when you inject entitlement and equity into the mix, there's always the question of why a person holds a particular position. Did they earn it, or are they sitting in that chair because of their sex? Men wonder if a woman is really qualified. Women wonder if a man is there only because he's privileged. Trust is severed. Bitterness builds. Women are unhappy. And men are silenced.

## WOMEN ARE BITCHY TOWARD ONE ANOTHER FOR A VERY NATURAL REASON.

Competition between men and women in the context of equality of outcomes, however, is only one reason women are difficult in the workplace. Another has to do with the nature of women and the outworking of that nature in a competitive sphere, particularly as women relate to one another. I worked for a media news outlet for several years in which writers talked frequently on message boards where we could share ideas and generate topics for articles. The writers at the company were divided into two groups—male and female. The men had their own message board and so did the women. The publisher believed it would be better to have them separate so the women's feelings wouldn't get hurt by thoughtless men, and so both groups could feel free to discuss intimate and personal issues without being exploited by the opposite sex. The arrangement didn't work out as well as the publisher planned. The men's message board was a breeze, as guys shared their dirty jokes and competed with one another. At the end of the day, they all virtually shook hands and went their merry way. Not so for the women. The female message board was the opposite. Bickering, fighting, backstabbing, mean-girl cliques, passive-aggressive landmines, gossiping, and hurt feelings that led to women quitting the message board, angry at the abuse they'd received from other women.

It wasn't like that every day, of course. We would have periods of peace when we'd be supportive of one another, laugh about what was going on in politics, and encourage those who were struggling. Women aren't always a pack of hyenas when they gather in a group. But it never lasted, and the women's message board rarely mirrored the peace and ease of the men's. I asked my fellow writers if they'd ever experienced this at other outlets, and they all agreed that they had observed similar behavior—and the more competitive, the worse it was. This phenomenon even extended outside the professional world. Women who attended all-female Bible studies complained that they would often be nasty to each other. Neighborhood women's groups would eventually devolve into backstabbing cliques warring over petty grievances.

What is wrong with women? I used to complain about them and tell friends, "I hate working with women. They can be such bitches!" Oddly, a lot of women felt the same. I can't tell you how many times I've heard women confess, "I prefer to work with men. They're so easy!" Most of us ladies admit we can be just as bitchy or problematic as other women. Maybe not in the same way or to the same degree—there are different types of women in the workplace, from the queen bee to the stealth bomber—but we certainly see ourselves in the mix. Some women, of course, are not as bad as others. Individual personality plays a role, and a woman who is not very competitive is typically the nicest in the bunch, but on the whole, women are trouble. Confessing that they're difficult in the workplace is kind of like a man admitting that he notices a woman's breasts. "It's our nature," they admit with a shrug and a sheepish smile, knowing that while this is certainly true, they can still make improvements—if they're honest with themselves.

But what does this mean—it's a woman's nature? Is it merely that they're more emotional than men? Women certainly process information differently than men, but being emotional can be an asset if it's channeled correctly. Emotional doesn't always equal irrational. Emotional doesn't always equal difficult. There's something deeper going on here that most women don't want to talk about—and most men won't because they're not allowed to say anything critical of the sisterhood. After observing this for years, especially in highly competitive arenas like political media, I decided to do some analysis of the situation rather than just chalking it up to women being nasty. I wanted to know *why* they're nasty. The answer is found in the depths of the female psyche, particularly in the context of competition, which is part and parcel of the professional world. Women compete very differently than men, and that difference is tied to their feminine nature. They don't compete objectively as a man does, which leaves all competition—especially competition that isn't objectively clear-cut—a highly personal endeavor that triggers natural feminine responses to challenges. This aspect of the feminine identity affects how women interact with both men and women in the workplace, and it is one of the primary reasons they can be so bitchy.

This book is about understanding our identity, not just as human beings or unique individuals, but as males and females (a point I explain in more detail in Chapter 9). That identity is designed for a purpose—a purpose expressed differently according to a person's individual design, yet still containing the common qualities of our sex. In other words, every individual is different, but every woman is the same in some ways—a shared identity that is very different from a man's. The individual traits, influences, personalities, pathologies, advantages, and so forth affect those common female traits, but they don't cause them to disappear. This intransigence of the feminine is why we can make generalities that are accurate and fair. Just as we don't stop being human, no matter how different we are as individuals, women don't stop being female. As females they are hardwired to interact with men and other women in particular ways. This doesn't mean they can't manage and redirect that wiring, but it is a part of them. To deny it is to fail to know themselves. The same is true of men.

## A woman measures her worth more in who she is than what she does.

A woman's identity as a female is a passive trait. Women don't prove their femininity. They don't earn passage into womanhood—their body does it for them through menstruation and, for some, childbirth. A woman's feminine nature isn't mainly in what she *does*, but in who she *is*. She identifies as a woman by her very being, not by her doing. This state of being is very different from a man. While a man is certainly masculine in his being, he shows his manhood—and his manhood is judged—according to what he does. He has rites of passage that involve doing, overcoming, conquering, achieving, and showing courage. This extends to how he interacts with the opposite sex. A man's relationship with a woman is very much active. He woos her not just by sitting there and looking handsome; he shows her his worth, his manhood, his value. This often involves competition with other men. Romantic literature is filled with tales of men competing for a woman's hand. Poetry is written to woo the woman. One of the main narratives in human existence is the man saving the damsel, beating back monsters, and earning her love. This is the man's natural role, and it's why attempts to make women the saviors of men in fiction fall flat. Men do the wooing and saving; women decide if they're worthy. Though all of our relationships are not erotic, these sexual dynamics undergird our interactions with the opposite sex in various ways—often without our even realizing it. We respond and react instinctively as men and as women. We like to pretend that we're suddenly androgynous when we step into the professional world, but we're always male and female with inherent differences and distinctiveness.

For example, while men are active in expressing their sexuality, women are not. A woman is active in other ways, but the expression of her femininity is essentially who she is, not what she does. She can distort that femininity and corrupt it, but the development and natural expression of it is passive. This is why you never hear, "Prove you're a woman," while it's quite common for men to be told to prove that they're real men. A woman's beauty, her disposition, her inner trait of gentleness, her emotional responses, and her power in giving birth—all, and more, comprise the feminine like a flower open to the light. Some might think birthing a baby is active. It's not really. The sex was active, but pregnancy is a state of being for the woman—a fact that makes her feel profoundly vulnerable. I don't know any woman who gets pregnant and gives birth to prove her feminine prowess to men. Once a woman chooses to get pregnant, no other real choices are involved—her body takes over.

Men like to praise women for their heroism in childbirth, and feminists like to talk about it too, including their courage to face bleeding every month. They love to yell about the bravery of bloody panties when they're rallying the troops for feminist causes.

But I'm going to be honest with you. Women don't have a choice! There's really nothing brave about it. When women bleed, it's an act of nature. When men bleed (usually on the battlefield), it's a choice—an act of love. My body started bleeding when I was twelve, whether I wanted it to or not. After I got married, I chose to have sex and, as a result, got pregnant, but once the pregnancy started, I just had to let it happen. When the birthing pains began and the water broke, I had to roll with it, carried along on the current of my feminine nature. I was crying and screaming and wishing I were anywhere else except lying on a table with my belly convulsing in waves of agonizing pain. Then the baby came and I thanked God it was over. My body had done its job.

This point is a bit of irony when abortion advocates talk about a forced pregnancy. A woman chooses to have sex knowing that, by the very act, it is possible to have a child. But then, when she gets pregnant, she acts as if something had been done *to* her. Unless she was raped, nothing has been done to her at all. She did it to herself when she chose to have sex. There is, however, a seed of truth in the "forced pregnancy" idea. Once you're pregnant, you're stuck with it. Your body is very much "doing something to you." But you are your body and your body is you, so, in essence, you are forcing pregnancy on yourself. Abortion advocates, however, act as if some outside force that denies them the right to kill the baby and end the pregnancy is forcing the pregnancy on them. Not so. External forces that want to make abortion illegal are only making women accountable for their own choices and responsibilities: to protect the life within no matter how difficult it is and to allow their bodies to do what they were designed to do. Ironically, if there is any bravery in pregnancy, it's in the woman who didn't want to get pregnant, faces the consequences of her own choices, and chooses to let nature take its life-forming course instead of ending it because she doesn't want to be "forced" by her own body to have a baby. The woman who gets an abortion in the name of pro-choice, instead, violates nature, actively enters into the sacred realm of her own body, and destroys the life she put there. Isn't it ironic that those who claim, "My body, my choice," are at war with their own bodies? Time and again, feminism butts its head against nature and finds it unrelenting.

Whether it's having babies, dating, or working in an office, women have a passivity that defines them. A woman is designed as a receiver. She is the goal, if you will, that the masculine moves to attract. This creates a uniquely competitive dynamic among women. The competition that women have with each other—as women—is not who can construct the best football game out of paper, who can climb the highest mountain, or who can build the best car from scratch. It's who *is* the best woman. Women fundamentally compete not by what they do, but by who they are. You might not be trying to catch and keep a man—you might be competing to get a coveted sales account or race to develop the best architectural plan—but a woman's instinct to identify herself as part of the competition is intrinsic to her nature. She can't remove herself from the equation unless she makes an effort through self-awareness—but even then, she'll still be a woman and not a man.

**In the midst of competition, women don't easily separate who they are from what they do.**

This feminine passivity doesn't mean women don't compete according to external performance. I played sports and competed in just about every competition imaginable when I was in school, from debate club to piano. I love to compete. That's my individual makeup. Still, my competitiveness as a woman is not quite the same as that of a man. This is especially true when the competition involves relational interaction, communication, formation of alliances, and self-presentation. By comparison, sports are more straightforward. You have a skill, and you win or you lose. I played soccer and ran track. When I played soccer, I was on a team with other girls (and, at times, boys too), and we had a single goal to perform physically. When I ran, I was competing purely on the ability to outrun my competition. Those competitors could have been aliens from another planet and not just other girls. The nature of the competitors didn't matter. It was only about the running and the mental focus to give it my all. This is one reason I love sports. There is clarity in the competition that I find refreshing, and also why it can't be compared to competition in the workplace.

Unless the workplace is very single-minded in production, and the competition is clear—like you see in sports—it is a more relational kind of competition. Promotions, for example, aren't always based on a number, a measurable skill, or particular merit—sometimes the person who is "best" at the task isn't promoted. Promotions and hiring, more often than not, involve a complex combination of factors. They're often heavily relational. In the context of this relational competition, the measures of success are not always easy to define. This isn't as much the case in the sciences, where accomplishments are measurable. But, even there, when you are dealing with hypotheses, vying for funding, and forming connections to convince others that your research is worthwhile, a subjectivity creeps into the process that results in relational competition.

This objective contest versus a more subjective one in any sphere brings out the differences between men and women like nothing else. This is because women compete subjectively while men compete objectively. The reason for this is rooted in the very nature of women. It's also why, even in female sports, women react within the competition much more defensively than men—think of the Tonya Harding affair with Nancy Kerrigan. When men compete, they measure their abilities, competency, and skill. This objective focus is true even in more subjective competitions like those in the workplace. The bottom line for men is, "Did I perform best?" Men have a detached attitude to competition that allows them to go out for a beer with the guy who just beat them in a fight. Unless they're extremely petty, undeveloped, immature in their masculinity, or unhealthy with low self-esteem, men can compete, lose—or win—and keep the relationships going. In other words, they don't take it personally. They lost or won, fair and square. It's something they did, not who they are.

For women, it's an entirely different story. In subjective competitions that are riddled with relationship intricacies, women aren't objective. They can be when it comes to the task—and they'll tell you that's their focus. But, in reality, there is another layer to a woman's competitive nature in these circumstances. She is not designed to compete with other women by what she does. She competes according to who she is. The context, for a woman, is always relational. When competition is injected into this relational dynamic, her identity is very much at stake. This is why a woman's looks are often discussed in the workplace. Just listen to commentary around the office—a woman's appearance will come up more than a man's.

This is one area where feminists ignoring innate differences between men and women is a problem. We are raising girls to compete like boys and failing to teach them to interact with women in a less competitive way or, at least, if they are competing against women, to understand how they're different. We need to teach girls to know themselves as females and to understand other women in the same way. They're not men, and the personal aspect of competition is always there—just under the surface. What we have now is women taught to compete like men, failing to do so, and creating conflict because they don't understand their own emotional responses. A woman's emotionality isn't the problem. At issue is her failure to understand why she emotes the way she does.

## Women use their feminine qualities to compete.

This subjective focus is why women revert to projecting their feminine traits in the workplace to exert power over men. Depending on their personalities and looks, they do this in a variety of ways. There's the vixen, who uses her sexuality to get ahead. This sexy persona doesn't mean she's sleeping with everyone. It means she's pretty enough to use it—the sexual beauty of a woman is very powerful and affects men. All women know this whether they want to admit it or not. Many act on it, some subtly, others shockingly overtly.

Other women choose to use feminine nurturing. They're the ones who emotionally—not necessarily sexually—position themselves in the office. They bring gifts to coworkers, encourage them when they're down, open their offices for therapy sessions, and make sure to praise those they work with to soothe them. I've seen this among female bosses. They'll flatter, encourage, and be sensitive in ways most men aren't. They compliment—a lot—at least those they like. This ability for women to use their feminine "wiles" in the workplace is, again, another trait that helps them to "compete." Healthy masculine men don't act like this. They're there to do a job.

Other women express their femininity by adopting an authoritarian-type role, which can be obnoxious when they take their place as the adult in the room, ruling the office like a matriarch, often forming a close-knit collection of men to surround them. You'll sometimes hear the men praising her for her "guy-like" qualities—that she isn't hampered by the emotionality of other women. She's "cool." What they don't realize is she has harnessed her own feminine energies to use as power over others. She's the one in control. She's above it all. She's the queen bee.

A perfect illustration of these dynamics between women in the workplace is a scene from the television series *Mad Men*. I realize this series is set in the '60s and '70s but, when it comes to how many women interact, not a lot has changed. One woman in the office, Peggy, worked her way up from secretary to the coveted position of a copywriter. She's the only woman in a high position at the advertising agency. Another woman in the office—Joan—is the office manager, the head secretary, if you will. Joan is a beautiful, sexy woman who uses her sexuality in all its glory, from sleeping with the boss to wearing accentuating clothing to show her curves. She's a combination of the vixen and the queen bee. One day, some of the men in the office posted a crude pornographic drawing of Joan on her office window. She is angry, of course, and takes down the picture.

Peggy is also offended, but she doesn't know what to do. The men who did it are her subordinates, but this is new territory for her. She goes to her boss, Don Draper, and tells him what happened. In typical male fashion, Don tells her to take control of the situation and fire the man who did it. He explains that he can't do it because then Peggy's authority would be weakened. She would be reduced to a tattletale who doesn't have the courage to fire her employees.

Both Peggy and Don are worried about what the men will think if Peggy does something. How wrong they were. On Don's advice, Peggy confronts the man who did it and fires him. He's angry, of course, but Peggy feels empowered by taking the reigns and standing for what's right. Afterward, she joins Joan in the elevator, expecting Joan to praise her for coming to her defense. The sisters should stick together, right? No. Joan is furious with Peggy. Joan's power in the office is how she manipulates men. She wanted to punish the creep in her own way, and she had a plan. Peggy ruined that by exerting her authority into the conflict, thereby weakening Joan's power in the office. Peggy failed to see how Joan's control was based on her femininity, and Peggy—another woman—stole that from her.

Later in the series, Joan goes so far as to sleep with a client to seal a deal for the company and elevate her position in the office. Don—infamous for womanizing—is surprisingly against it, wanting her to elevate herself through hard work and not demean herself with sex. Though Joan is initially offended at the prospect of sleeping with the client—since it was first suggested by a man in the office—she complied. She used her ultimate weapon, sex, to secure a powerful place in the company. I wish I could say this is just fiction or a thing of the past, but it is a lot more common today than feminists want to admit. I'd also go so far as to say that a lot of #MeToo incidents arise from women playing the sex card and not liking the outcome.

## MEN HAVE CHANGED FOR WOMEN, BUT WOMEN HAVEN'T CHANGED THEMSELVES.

Women are different from men—it's as simple as that. Looks and appearances are more relevant for women. Take, for example, the business in which I work. A female media broadcaster is judged not only by her abilities, but also by her appearance. Women who are ugly, old, and haggard aren't deemed as appealing as young, blonde, blue-eyed, shapely hotties. This judgment extends even to her attitude. Have you ever noticed that a temperamental man who unleashes on television is judged less harshly than a cold, angry woman who does the same? There is a tacit admission in all these judgments that the woman is acting contrary to her more refined feminine disposition. It's the same reason a woman cursing is more jarring than a man doing the same. She is being judged according to who she is, not merely what she does.

I know, I know. This focus on the subjective seems terribly unfair, and it's something feminists have battled for decades. Judge a woman on her merit, not on her subjective qualities. Judge her as you would a man. The irony is that men have tried—though certainly not all—but it's not just men who need to make an effort; women need to make changes too—including recognizing and taking responsibility for how they compete in the workplace. The real problem feminists have when it comes to these dynamics in the workplace is not with men, but with other women.

When women criticize and compete with other women, their identity as a woman is on the line. If they lose in these subjective situations, it cuts deep. They feel like they have been rejected, that the lesser woman won, that their very selves have been cast aside. This is why the emotional levels among women rise when they're in a competitive situation. Consider the message board at the online magazine where I worked. The men sought camaraderie and enjoyed it. When they did compete with one another, either through debate or for a chance to write a post on a particular topic, they did it objectively. Does this mean some men didn't get their feelings hurt and take it personally? Of course. But, generally, they were more relaxed in the conflict and confident because the innate sense of competition they carried around within was objective.

The women, however, were thrown into a situation in which they were told to act like a team yet still compete with each other in an entirely self-interested way. This plan was nonsensical. Women can certainly work as a team toward a common goal—as the U.S. women's soccer team did when they defeated one team after another to win the World Cup. Women can also work together noncompetitively. When I worked in ministry, women gathered together to organize gifts for the poor, make food for the elderly, and organize children's ministries. In service, women typically work well together if they stay focused on the group task instead of spiraling into petty competitions. As Brick observed, women can find the silliest things to compete about—and it's because their identity is at stake. This is why it's important to remain as objective as possible; as soon as subjective competition is added to the mix, conflict flares that cuts to the core of a woman's feminine identity.

In the case of the message board at the magazine where I worked, women were competing with each other at a high level to be selected for television, radio, podcasts, stories, and placement on the website. Yet they were told to work together as a team when there wasn't really a team, just as there wasn't any real common goal aside from soldiering on as fellow combatants in the culture war and ensuring success of the magazine. These lofty goals, however, paled when direct competition for work and notoriety defined the ethos of the women's message board. The only functional team might have comprised a few staff members who worked together, but the rest of us were fighting for positioning in a profession in which many factors came together to form the competition, including how we looked, presented ourselves, and related to others in a way that promoted one's position. This subjective competition was so strong that even momentary alliances and friendships broke under the weight of it when women found themselves at odds with former allies. The teamwork was a mirage of vicious competition that resulted in outcasts, occasional peacemakers, traitors, and coalitions formed to knock down unapproved threats to the status of those in a more powerful position. Any slight became personal; some felt it more keenly than others, depending on how secure they were in themselves and their position. One woman might have felt judged of her intellect, another her looks, another her insight, another her intuition. Whatever it was, the women took it personally. This outcome was inevitable, considering the female nature.

It would have helped a great deal to have men included in the mix—co-contributors, not just one or two men in authority who already interacted on the women's message board occasionally. The presence of male bosses who made ultimate judgments about the ladies' professional fates just added to the conflict as women vied for attention and jealousies arose as they sought to stand out from the crowd. An infusion of masculinity on a broader scale, however, would have been beneficial. Despite the natural tension a man brings to a brood of females, women usually do much better competing with men in the workplace than with other women. When a woman competes directly with a man, she still takes it personally, but he tempers her with his objectivity.

Brick tried this with her female-only company when she decided to infuse the office with some testosterone to keep the business afloat. The result wasn't surprising. "The team suddenly became quieter, more hard-working and less bitchy—partly because they were too busy flirting…each out to prove that they were the sexiest in the room."[36] Okay, maybe it wasn't a panacea—women love to compete for a man's attention even in the most nonsexual environments. Jealousies and envy inevitably poke through the professional veneer, but at least there was some measure of calm with the male additions. Brick's experience—like my own—is just more proof that sexuality is ingrained in our psyche.

Men calm the savage beast that is a woman in a subjective competitive atmosphere, but when women compete only against other women, there's no one to temper them. They can become like crazed harpies as they stand toe to toe competing not only by what they do, but who they are. This increases the stakes and emotions. You can't as easily shake hands after you've lost to another woman unless you force yourself to focus on the objective—and, if there's not much objectivity in the competition, it's nearly impossible.

Women will deny this is true, but those of us who are honest about ourselves and our experiences will admit it.

The competition—no matter how professional and nonromantic—slices too closely into a woman's basic feminine nature in which she "wins" by being *who she is* in all her glory. It taps into her instinct to protect her man and her relationships. It threatens her status as the only *one* that was chosen above all others. Every other woman is a wolf seeking to invade her home and steal her man. This is her gut impulse, even if she doesn't express it or know it. Such an invasion can't be tolerated. A woman is designed to be chosen by a man above all other women by the sheer power of her presence. To have that challenged is an existential conflict, and that nature is always lingering in the back of her mind, subconscious but powerful. This urge is mitigated, to a greater or lesser degree, if she is rooted in a stable relationship in which her need to feel chosen is well established or if for some other reason—usually spiritual—she is profoundly secure in herself without getting enmeshed in the competition. But even with this personal anchor, a woman acting in a competitive environment will still look into the glass of competition as a mirror in which her identity is reflected. It's natural.

This personalization of the feminine doesn't mean every woman who competes and loses in the workplace melts into a pile of goo crying about her self-esteem. I'm not talking about self-worth being on the line. This isn't about ego in the psychological sense. I'm talking about how the dynamic of a woman's sense of competition born of her sexual nature impacts her performance, attitudes, and relations at work. Even in tough-girl roles on television, this sexual nature seeps through. In the early days of *NCIS*, the male lead criticized a female agent under his command for something she did wrong. "I'm not stupid," she replied. He coolly responded, "Never said you were."[37] She took the criticism, the "failure" in the competition of work, as a personal judgment. He was simply criticizing what she had done. A male employee would not have responded the way she did. He'd either take the rebuke or argue that he didn't do what the boss said he did. They'd hash it out and go their separate ways without either thinking the other assumed he was "stupid."

## MEN ARE FILLED WITH A WONDER THAT GUIDES THEIR ROLE AS PROVIDER.

Women not only need to be honest with themselves about how they act in the workplace, but they also need to understand how men act, what motivates them, and where they get their satisfaction. Men, for example, would prefer to be active doing a task rather than having one meeting after another, discussing what might be done. This doesn't mean meetings aren't necessary, but women tend to make them a lot more important than they are. Ask most men what they'd rather be doing in the office; it won't be sitting around discussing ideas. If a meeting is necessary, they want to get it done efficiently and quickly so they can move along to the task at hand. Instead of forcing men to sit down and act like women in the workplace, women—especially female bosses—need to respect how a man performs best and let him do it.

While women certainly enjoy developing their skills and becoming competent in their jobs, there is an innate sense of wonder within a man when it comes to learning, growing, inventing, creating, and exploring that women often underappreciate. Men want to tend to the task at hand, and the last thing mature, masculine men want is to be entangled in the competitive snares of bitchy women in the workplace.

The Jungian masculine archetype that embodies this sense of the man is the *magician*—"the knower" and "the master of technology," Moore and Gillette write in *King, Warrior, Magician, Lover.*[38] This aspect of the male psyche seeks knowledge and wants to uncover the secrets of the universe. A man longs to understand not just how things work but why, and he loves to develop his mind and abilities to explore new boundaries and discover new ways of doing things. As the magician (also known as a sage or prophet), men are seeking to become masters at their trade, and they find deep satisfaction in it. Moore and Gillette give a wonderful description of a man's need to explore the secrets of life:

> Whether you are an apprentice training to become a master electrician, unraveling the mysteries of high voltage; or a medical student, grinding away night and day, studying the secrets of the human body and using the available technologies to help your patients; or a would-be stockbroker or a student of high finance; or a trainee in one of the psychoanalytic schools, you are in exactly the same position as the apprentice shaman or witch doctors in tribal societies. You are spending large amounts of time, energy, and money in order to be initiated into rarefied realms of secret power. You are undergoing an ordeal testing your capacities to become a master of this power. And, as is true in all initiations, there is guarantee of success.[39]

Life is a mysterious adventure for men. They want to unlock its secret doors and step through them to discover new worlds of thought and action. Women would help men greatly if they recognized this deep need and desire within the masculine soul. Men aren't just toiling away to pay the bills—though they are certainly doing this, and not all jobs are interesting. But every healthy male wants to find meaning in his work, to have his mind broadened, and to contribute something to the world. He needs to be active—not just talk about other people's ideas. He wants to find his own and put his hands to work molding and shaping them into reality.

When a man is inspired and unleashed from the control of women, he will go to great lengths in his work. He'll put himself at risk, shock the world with his unconventional approaches to solve problems, and take risks to overcome obstacles. The scientist in the laboratory will work tirelessly to find elegant proof of his hypothesis. The teacher will use his intuition and insight to inspire his students to achieve greater heights. The marketing director will develop new plans to reach more people with creativity that is often suppressed while running from one meeting to another.

I'm not saying women aren't motivated by the wonder of discovery and knowledge. They are—and the contributions women have made are manifold. But women often forget how men are driven by these desires in their own unique ways. As little boys, they played in the woods for hours building forts and fashioning weapons. As men, they're looking to the skies to build space stations and pave pathways to the stars.

A man's work is rarely ever for himself alone—which is why it hurts him so deeply when it's abused or unappreciated. It's not just about proving himself for the admiration of others or to make money—though these are certainly part of it. There is a necessity to work that is undeniable. But work is also a service—for his family and for his world. He seeks personal achievement, but he is satisfied in his masculine soul by so much more—by making a difference through using his mind and his hands to create a better life for others.

It doesn't take much to inspire a man, to set him loose like a wild horse to run like the wind. When he knows his labor is constructive, when it is appreciated and benefits others who respect him for his excellence, he is deeply satisfied and inspired to do even more. Will he do it even without the appreciation? Most will. That's what men do—they push through—but they are happier and more content when they are respected for their work. They're designed to accomplish for others, not just for themselves, and they are content when gratitude is given. If women love the men in their lives, they'll want them to be happy and not treat them merely as an ATM. If both work professional jobs, the woman will appreciate her husband's accomplishments as much as her own. She'll show respect rather than taking him for granted.

Unlike women who can create within themselves as part of their internal energies, a man creates solely outside of himself. He needs to outwardly express this creativity and strive to become masters in whatever field he has chosen. To watch that inner desire blossom in a man is a wonder in itself. I love to watch my husband work on a project. He has very artistic hands, and he handles equipment with intuitive knowledge. Like many men, he enjoys guns, not just developing the skill of shooting them, but learning about them, examining how they function, looking for ways to improve the original design. Nothing impresses my husband more than a machine that is elegantly designed, functional but with a simplicity that is genius. He is always looking for ways to improve how something works, whether it's guns, knives, cameras, or tools. As he works on them, he goes somewhere else in his mind, imagining what he wants and seeking ways to make it a reality. It's a beautiful thing to watch, and I find myself caught up in his wonder. I also find myself falling deeper in love with him. Men are truly magical.

When my son was little, he would spend hours alone building Lego sets and drawing imaginary creatures for a world of his own making. I would watch him as he carefully thought through every creation, adding details here and there until he got it just right. Later, when he was in middle school, he discovered the wonders of science and joined the Science Olympiad team, in which students compete to win medals as the most knowledgeable in a given category. My son excelled at rocks and minerals, reptiles and amphibians, and food science. He researched each topic, filling notebooks with what he had learned. With each discovery, his face would brighten, and when he'd take home a gold medal in an event, tears of pride would brim in his eyes.

When my son graduated from high school, he knew exactly what he was going to do—go to college and earn degrees in microbiology and biochemistry. He accomplished his goals and took the next step to get his doctorate to become a research scientist. Today, he spends hours in his lab studying HIV and looking for a creative way to kill this deadly virus. My son isn't a warrior in the classic sense, but he is a living, breathing example of the magician archetype. Like Dr. Spencer Reid of *Criminal Minds*, his contribution to the betterment of society comes from the excellence of his mind. He's a warrior of creativity and invention. Many men in many professions are doing this every day, but not all are appreciated for their efforts.

A man in the workplace is not only laboring to provide for his family—an essential aspect of the male identity. He is also setting out to conquer something. Women don't typically think of their work as "conquering," but this is precisely what it is for a man. He's expressing himself, competing, and providing, but he is also overcoming life's obstacles to make life better. This aspect of manliness is rooted in God's design for men to cultivate this planet for good, not merely for selfish gain. By working, a man is providing, he's nurturing, he's giving, he's overcoming—and this brings him deep satisfaction and joy.

Too many men are struggling because they have lost their purpose in the workplace. They are herded into meeting rooms like women, told to cooperate like women, expected to treat women as men even though they don't act like it, ignored when they come home, and told they must provide for others even when others don't appreciate it. Their role in the workplace is reduced to pure necessity, devoid of the power and wonder that comes from a man seeking excellence, exercising dominion over his environment, and serving through creativity. This has a dehumanizing and emasculating effect on men, who derive so much satisfaction from their magical role as provider. Women could go a long way in helping men excel if they would let men be men in the workplace.

Instead of seeing men as mere competition or failures because they're not acting like women, they need to be free to explore the forests, uncover rocks just to see what's there, dismantle the old television or broken car and rebuild it as something better, or simply spend time alone unlocking the mysteries of life. If a woman respects a man's world of discovery, he will move mountains for her.

CHAPTER 5

# MEN AS KINGS (WOMEN STEAL THE SCEPTERS)

*It is a glorious thing to stablish peace, / And kings approach the nearest unto God / By giving life and safety unto men.*

—Shakespeare, *King Edward III*

My mom called me early in the morning, frantic and nearly hysterical. My seventy-eight-year-old father, who had been in the hospital due to a blood clot, had become dehydrated and malnourished because the local hospital had failed to care for him. He was delirious, reliving days in Vietnam, yelling orders to troops, lashing out in terror at unseen enemies. I told my mother to do whatever was possible to get him out of there and take him to another hospital where he could get better care. She hired a private ambulance service, and despite protests from nurses, transported him to a hospital two hours away.

I got in my car and traveled from Charlotte to the coast, hoping that, by the time I got there, my dad would be stabilized. I wasn't prepared for what I found. My Marine father, once vibrant, strong, in command, and full of life, wasn't himself. Lying in the bed was a man I didn't recognize. His cheeks were sunken, his eyes swollen, his hair tangled, his skin a pale gray; he seemed unable to catch his breath, and he kept pulling oxygen tubes away from his nose. Worse was the wild look in his eyes as they darted from one point to another, seeing things only he could see.

I hurried to his bedside. He turned as I touched his shoulder.

"Hello," he said slowly, as if he were trying to remember something from long ago.

I took his hand and held it. "Hi, Dad," I managed. He lifted his head to give me a kiss. His lips were cracked with drool crusted in the corners. I didn't hesitate for a second and kissed him. "How are you?" I asked.

"The reports need to be filed, and then we need to get out of here," he said with a strained voice as he pointed to something in the far corner of the room. "There's the patrol…we need to find it and take care of business." He squeezed my hand, his eyes wide. He motioned for me to come closer. "Not many make it out," he whispered.

"We'll get out, Dad; don't worry," I whispered back. He nodded and started pulling at his IV. My mom told him to stop, but he didn't listen. He kept trying to grab the tube. I moved his hand away, and he started fumbling with the blanket that was draped over him. He seemed to be looking for something. "What are you looking for?" I asked.

"My jacket…the button," he said. He was getting agitated.

I lifted the blanket and pretended to find the button on his imaginary jacket. "Here it is," I said.

He reached to take it. "Thank you." He looked at the invisible button between his fingers, let out a slow breath, and turned away, talking to someone about getting men off the flight deck.

"He's at least calmer now," my mom said as she sank into a chair. She glanced at our hands and smiled. "It's because you're here."

I tried to talk to him, but he didn't seem to know I was there any longer, even though he was still holding my hand.

Looking at our hands reminded me of a time when I was young, when my dad taught me to swim. He didn't do it like most dads. Often there were no water wings, no shallow ends of the swimming pool. My dad took me to the beach on the Marine Corps base, put me on a boogie board, pulled me out just beyond the waves, and told me to get off. I was terrified, but I obeyed. I gasped for air as I flailed in the water, desperately trying to feel the sand beneath my toes as the tide fell. From a few feet away, my dad yelled at me to kick my legs. But I couldn't. I was too weak and too afraid. I was going to drown. The tide lifted, filling my mouth and nose with water. I tried to kick, but the tide rolled over me. Just as I went under, I felt my dad grab hold of my hand. "You can do it," he said. He held me at arm's length, so I could kick. The tide rose, and salt stung my eyes, but I wasn't afraid any longer. My dad was there. He wouldn't let me drown. He wouldn't let me go.

As I stood beside my dad's hospital bed, the scent of salt in the ocean air and the crash of waves faded, replaced by the bitter smell of ammonia and the whoosh and beeps of hospital machines. I held tightly to his hand, leaned over, and kissed his cheek. "You can do it," I whispered.

Two days later, I had to leave to go home. For the next couple of weeks, doctors worked on my dad's recovery. My mom stayed with him, going back home only when she needed supplies. She was tired, and the stress was taking its toll. When she called me to give me an update but could barely talk because of the tears, I knew

I had to leave my work and family responsibilities. My parents needed me. Despite my turbulent upbringing, littered with fear and abuse born of my father's own suffering, I knew my parents loved me. I knew my dad loved me.

I could see it in his eyes when he would take me to the beach in the evenings, and, as the stars appeared, he'd set up his telescope and tell me about constellations and the possibility of life on other planets. We would usually go in the fall when nights were cool, and a soft wind blew in from the ocean. He'd make a small fire, and we would eat MREs—military meals ready to eat. I loved the crackers in the green cans and the chocolate bars that melted in my mouth. As the fire crackled and waves crashed, and as the breeze rushed through sea grasses, my father would tell me adventures from his travels. I sat fascinated, nibbling on smoked cheese, as he described a leader of a desert tribe ride into the Marine Corps base camp on a beach in Iran where they were surveying the land. My dad was a telegraphic surveyor and would be stationed on beachheads for months making maps for future landings. In full regalia of golden robes, the man swept in on a white horse without saying a word. From beneath his head wrap, he looked at the men, his dark eyes the most piercing my dad had ever seen. After a few tense moments, he turned and rode off in a cloud of sand, never speaking to a soul. My dad shook his head at the memory, impacted in a way I didn't understand by that brief encounter with a powerful foe. I was awestruck, captivated by my father's words. I felt, in those moments, like there was no one else in the world. Just the two of us and the stars.

As I made my way across the bleakness of Eastern North Carolina, passing cotton fields, rows of pine trees, and camouflage trucks with dead bucks strapped to the front bumper, I tried to distract myself from the worry. I shuffled through my iPod. I talked to friends on the phone. I listened to the news. But my heart was heavy. Would my dad recognize me? Would he ever be strong enough to go home? Would we ever walk along the beach again and watch sunlight dance on the waves?

When I walked into the hospital, I found my father sitting up, his eyes bright, his skin full of color. "Denise!" he said, his smile big. He held open his arms for me to come to him. I hurried over and gave him a hug and a kiss. He pulled me close, his white beard tickling my cheek. "It's good to see you, darling," he said.

Tears streamed down my face, the taste of saltwater on my lips. "It's always good to see you, Dad."

Children need their fathers. I know I needed mine. I needed him to pull me from my dreamy world and teach me to work hard even when I didn't feel like it. I needed him to discipline me when I lied or tried to sneak out at night with friends—especially when those nights transformed into a drunken foray. I needed him to force me to do my homework and try to find answers on my own without him or my mother making it easy for me. I needed him to challenge me to enter piano competitions even when I was so nervous I wanted to vomit before going on stage. I needed him to teach me to play basketball in the backyard when we competed with my older brother in games of HORSE. I needed him to help me push through pain, to survive, to accept defeat with grace but never to give up. I needed him to wrap his arms around me to show me the security of a man's love.

I needed my mother too but in a different way, in a softer frame in which I learned female strength. But fathers are a unique force unto themselves, and children need that connection and love. They need their father's encouragement, protection, and sense of order. They are our guides as we navigate life to find our place in the world. They do it imperfectly. They make mistakes. They can be selfish at times. They can cause pain. They are human, after all. But a father's heart is designed to love and cherish those in his care. His leadership forms the foundation of the family, and the family is the foundation of society. Without it, without fathers, we all suffer.

When I talk to men about what they want to say to women, I inevitably get a host of comments about fatherhood and divorce. Even men who aren't divorced feel that their role as father is not respected.

"Men need to parent their children without Mom getting in the way all the time."

"Don't refer to me as 'babysitting' the kids when you go out. No, I'm their father. I'm co-parenting."

"Wives need to trust their husbands to raise their sons even when it makes them uncomfortable."

"If I'm the father of the child you're carrying, I have just as much say in that child's future as you do. We both played a part in creating that child, and we should both have equal say in whether that child lives or not."

"I am not just an ATM for our kids. As a divorced dad, I have a right to see my children and develop a relationship with them that's beyond giving them money."

"The courts need to stop assuming dad is irrelevant. We're just as important as moms, and the courts should recognize that."

"I'm not a freakin' loser like those dads on television. Stop treating me that way."

"Nothing irritates me more than sitting in church and dads being treated as if they're the problem. Everyone's always afraid to offend the women—as if they're innocent. That's not always the case."

"Boys need their dads to be strong, to teach them how to be men. Women simply can't do it the way a dad can."

> "The man is the head of the home, and he needs to act like it. Women need to accept it. When he rules over the home kingdom in love—everyone is better off."

## MEN LEAD BY ACTIVELY ORDERING THEIR HOMES AND THE WORLD.

A man's purpose is to bring order, keep his loved ones safe, make sure they are provided for, and train children to be organized in a chaotic world. He is king of his kingdom, ruling along with his queen for the good of those in his realm. "The King archetype in its fullness possesses the qualities of order, of reasonable and rational patterning, of integration and integrity in the masculine psyche," authors Moore and Gillette explain.

> It stabilizes chaotic emotion and out-of-control behaviors. It gives stability and centeredness. It brings calm. And in its "fertilizing" and centeredness, it mediates vitality, life-force, and joy. It brings maintenance and balance. It defends our own sense of inner order, our own integrity of being and of purpose, our own central calmness about who we are, and our essential unassailability and certainty in our masculine identity. It looks upon the world with a firm but kindly eye. It sees others in all their weakness and in all their talent and worth. It honors them and promotes them. It guides them and nurtures them toward their own fullness of being. It is not envious, because it is secure, as the King, in its own worth. It rewards and encourages creativity in us and in others.[40]

A man's most noble responsibility is to raise children who will grow to be free and responsible members of society. He teaches them to be self-controlled, to order themselves, to know their purpose in life, and to develop logical minds and courageous hearts—without which they can't bring order to anything else. He is key to discovering their identity and taking that self-awareness into every sphere of life with confidence.

Unfortunately, the unique purposes of a father are often unappreciated in our society—and even maligned. This was evident recently when a video of football player Tom Brady "cliff-diving" with his six-year-old daughter went viral. As if it were any of their business, viewers criticized him for putting his daughter at risk and being irresponsible. The cliff wasn't very high—I would hardly call it cliff-diving, which has a connotation of great height—but it was admittedly somewhat dangerous. The faint-hearted screamed and protested, failing to appreciate the differing ways fathers parent their children. Brady was right there with her. He didn't leave her side. They were having fun. It was risky, but he was there to pull her up and swim with her to the shore. I'm sure his daughter will carry his bravery with her for the rest of her life. In that moment, he taught her to conquer her fears. I admit, as a mom, I wouldn't have had the nerve to do that, and I'd probably be standing there with my hands clenched and my heart pounding with nerves. But a dad needs to be a father to show his children the world in a way a mother never will. The last thing a child needs is two mommies.

A man's way of training children is different from a mother's because his masculine nature is different, and he affects his children in their development as only he can—sometimes that involves cliff-diving, climbing trees, and jumping off a surfboard past the ocean waves. To lose the father in the home is to lose its center, its source of masculine courage, and its order—it robs children of the primary source of self-knowledge, confidence, and awareness of their purpose as human beings and their design as males and females.

A woman, by the sheer nature of her body, creates within herself. She brings order to the world by her being, not merely by her doing. She soothes, civilizes, nurtures, and shapes others by her presence. Have you ever seen a group of men hanging around, telling jokes, acting as men do, but, when a woman walks in, they immediately shape up and tone down what they're saying? They might not know the woman, but her feminine presence brings a sense of order to their lives.

One of the travesties of modern feminism with its demand that women be treated just like men, that women invade men's spaces and act like one of the guys, and that men look at women as fellow men instead of the glorious females they are, is a coarsening of interactions between men and women. The irony is that when this happens, women complain that men are toxic and that they aren't respectful to the women in their presence, so they try to change men and redefine "men's spaces," making them more like a woman's. This leaves men confused. They're told on the one hand that they need to treat women equally, but on the other that when women enter their space, they have to treat them differently—as women.

So which is it? Some women would claim that men should always behave civilly, but this ignores the unique qualities of men as they interact with one another. Men should be free to be rough and irreverent when they're in a group. They don't need their spaces to be "female approved," and they should be able to keep signs on tree-house doors that say "No Girls Allowed." It's how they bond, how they sharpen each other, and how they validate one another's manhood. They have their own humor, their own way of analyzing situations, and their shared adoration of feminine beauty, which they inevitably recognize and comment on—sometimes in not-so-subtle tones. Men have their way of bringing order among men, but it's not how women do it. They do it actively, through competition and male cooperation. They're gritty, dirty, and sometimes crude. If they're out of the line of male decency, they hold one another to account. Men have their ways of keeping order in the pack. Women, however, bring a completely different dimension to social interactions. They do this with their refined presence, their ability to influence with keen insight, and their intuitive understanding of relationships. They bear and raise children, taming men with the responsibilities of family. Men, on the other hand, *actively* bring order. Women are active as well through their work and creativity—one of my goals in writing this book is to bring order to chaos. But this is a *choice* women make. They have the luxury of being passive or active in bringing about change, but the fundamental quality of their femininity is passive order.

Men, on the other hand, must rule over their "kingdoms" outwardly, bringing order to chaos and bearing fruit through action because this is all they can do. It is what they are called to do, and they do it in their unique way. Women need to let fathers lead as they are designed, not as women want them to be. Leading and reflecting God's masculine image as a dynamic ruler is essential to their masculine nature. Living out that nature in the home is essential for children, and, sadly, too many children don't experience it.

## FATHERLESSNESS IS A DISEASE IN CIVILIZED SOCIETY.

The loss of fathers in the home is a national blight. I don't say tragedy because it is often purposely done. We divorce, we have children out of wedlock and refuse to get married, and we have children through sperm donors, intentionally depriving them of their father—the most important man in their life and essential for their development. It's a tragedy when "father deprivation" happens by accident through loss or unplanned pregnancies that simply can't result in marriage, but to purposely rob children of their father through hostile divorces, abandonment, alienation, or planned pregnancies with sperm purchases is cruel to children who are designed to be in relation with their biological father. Contrary to popular belief, the children are not all right when they're deprived of their father.

One of the most horrific trends of our times is single women (and men, though this is rare) and homosexual couples using sperm donors and surrogates to have children. I'm not referring to adoption or children who are the result of a divorce, but to the creation of a child with the *calculated intention* of denying that child a relationship with his or her mother or father. This preemptive abandonment is cruel to children whose needs and feelings are sacrificed so that adults can have their own emotional needs met through the contrived construction of a "new family." The undeniable truth is children need their biological parents, and this kind of forced social reconstruction is not creating a new family but perverting it.

I confess I have played my part in the decline of the family, having sought divorce nearly twenty years ago. It divided our family and robbed my children of necessary time with their father. The only thing I can say in my defense is that I did try to maintain the relationship between my children and their dad, no matter how difficult. For some time, I had them during the week and he had them every weekend. This seemed to help them maintain the relationship they needed with their father, though it was hardly optimal. Even when my ex-husband and I moved, we traveled every week to keep this arrangement until he relocated to the same city. The every-weekend schedule continued until family dynamics changed for my ex-husband, but even then he saw them as frequently as he could. Still, it wasn't ideal, and, as it was with my children, too many suffer in broken homes, unable to be with one parent or the other when they need them. Some divorced couples strive to maintain these relationships, but some don't because they allow personal feelings and anger to disrupt what's important for the children; women are particularly guilty of this. According to statistics gathered by the U.S. government, women are more prone to keep fathers from seeing their children than vice versa.

My current husband, who is also divorced, experienced this firsthand. Many years ago, he and I sifted through trash bags he had gathered from outside his ex-wife's house to find information that would help us reestablish visitation that had been disrupted by the mother. We couldn't believe what we found. A locket my husband gave to his daughter with both their pictures inside. A registration form for Boy Scouts with his son's last name changed from McAllister to the new stepfather's surname. A card from my husband to his oldest daughter, ripped in two, dividing the words "I love you always, Dad." Not many people fighting for custody can obtain such hard evidence of alienation (and there was more), but we stooped to the level of stealing trash to find it. We had to. His ex-wife wouldn't communicate with him. His three children were taken out of state without his permission, their last names changed, and their visitation cut to nonexistence without any legal foundation for future visits. Too many men have lived this nightmare, and the courts allow it to happen.

No matter the circumstances of any divorce, beyond abuse, children should not be deprived of their father or mother. The problem with divorce is that it creates distrust where there should be trust, insecurity where there should be safety, and hostility where there should be peace. The children didn't choose to have their parents divorce. They didn't have a say in being separated for periods from the two people who are foundational to their sense of self and security. Home should be a refuge, but divorce makes it a battlefield with the children caught running from one side to the other hoping not to get hit by the arrows the two sides are shooting. Divorce is one of my greatest regrets in my life. I never had to suffer through a child custody battle as my current husband did, but there were still plenty of conflicts and too many shots across a field where children had little protection.

I am in the odd position of seeing divorce from a couple of different angles. I am a mom who is divorced; I know what it's like to be in the woman's position. I can attest to how the courts favor women, how women take advantage of stereotypes against men, and how men aren't always the victims. Angry, frustrated, and too willing to give up putting forth the effort to be with their children and instead choosing to pour all their emotional and financial resources into a new wife and new children, men sometimes shirk their responsibilities, blaming the ex-wife for decisions they alone made as they are unable to adjust to a new situation.

I am also a stepmom of three children and am married to a man who went through a hellish custody battle. He had false accusations of abuse leveled against him and was deprived of seeing his children under those false accusations. He watched helplessly as the trust and love he once saw in his children's eyes fade as they parroted the words of adults with an agenda that my husband was no longer their "real dad," that he was "of the devil," and that they were "in danger" in his wicked household. Unwilling to give up, he fought for them, plunging us into debt and emotional turmoil. But he wasn't willing to be cast from their lives. He was their father, and if he wouldn't fight for them who would?

I won't go into any more details. You get the picture. The children are grown now, but they still don't like to hear about the conflicts. Loyalty to biological parents runs deep, and, as my stepdaughter told both her parents and stepparents when she was older, "I don't want to hear you say anything negative about the other parent." We've tried to abide by her wishes. What I have related here is a matter of record, due to the court case we all endured, and I believe it's important to tell you my experiences because I can relate to wives and husbands on all sides. I have been both the perpetrator and victim in divorce. I've felt empowered and helpless. Most of all, I've seen the effect it has on the children. While amicable divorces can help mitigate the pain of divorce, the children are still caught in a broken situation. They have to form new attachments to men and women they aren't biologically related to. They are still deprived of seeing their parents any time they want, and the security of experiencing the love of a mom and dad for each other is lost.

## FATHERLESS HOMES ARE DEVASTATING TO CHILDREN.

Nothing offends fathers more than Mom serving as a gatekeeper between them and their children. "Does Mom approve?" is like fingernails across a chalkboard. The denigration of fathers has been decades in the making, resulting in 50 percent of mothers seeing no value in a father having contact with his children after divorce.[41] When feminism turned from equality before the law to an attack on the family, fathers became the target. Pop culture became riddled with images of dad as the joke of the family. The Netflix series *Stranger Things* is one example, portraying the dad as a powerless dimwit who is constantly dismissed by the "wiser," emotionally in-touch mother. Even more offensive is being deprived of access to children altogether.

The removal of fathers has had tragic results on American culture. Not all of this is women's fault, of course. There are deadbeat dads aplenty. Both are guilty of contributing to the crisis. According to the U.S. Census Bureau, nearly twenty million children—that's one in four—don't have a father in the home.[42] Research abounds on how children need their *biological* father, and, without him, they face struggles other children don't. They are four times more likely to be poor, and girls are seven times more likely to become pregnant as teenagers. Children are more likely to face abuse and child neglect, do drugs, become alcoholics, struggle with obesity, commit crimes, and drop out of high school.

Girls without a relationship with their biological father don't do as well in school and are more likely to be sexually promiscuous. According to the U.S. Department of Health/Census, 63 percent of youth suicides are from homes without a biological dad. That's five times the national average. Ninety percent of children who run away from home and end up homeless on the streets are from fatherless homes—thirty-two times the average. Most male teenagers and men who commit mass shootings are the products of fatherless homes or divorce. After each horrific shooting, America plunges into a political debate about guns, failing to face up to the root problem that festers in the unstable psyche of these men—broken homes and lost relationships with a strong father. America has had periods in its history when guns were numerous—even with teens having rifles in their cars when they went to school. All this happened without the mass shootings we see today. The change has been the decline of the family and the loss of fathers who discern trouble in their children, take action to deal with it, and create a secure, identity-building, and others-focused environment for children to become stable members of society.

Another issue that devolves into useless political debate is rape and sexual assault. We hear a lot of complaints from feminists about men being sexually abusive, and they look to government to do something about it beyond enforcing laws, but it is masculinity modeled by dads that keeps boys from growing up to be sexually abusive. Nearly 80 percent of rapists with deep-seated anger issues come from homes with absent fathers. Fathers are often the focus of child abuse, but, according to U.S. government research, children are at a higher risk of abuse in single-parent households (which are mostly single mothers—only 18 percent of single-parent homes are men). The rate of child abuse in single-parent households is 27.3 children per thousand compared to 15.5 per thousand in a two-parent household.[43]

When it comes to divorce statistics, you can see why men are frustrated and angry about the prejudice leveled against them. As reported by the U.S. Department of Health and Human Services, fathers are vilified by family courts in just about every metric.

- 79.6 percent of custodial mothers receive a support award
- 29.9 percent of custodial fathers receive a support award
- 46.9 percent of non-custodial mothers totally default on support
- 26.9 percent of non-custodial fathers totally default on support
- 20 percent of non-custodial mothers pay support at some level
- 61 percent of non-custodial fathers pay support at some level
- 66.2 percent of single custodial mothers work less than full time
- 10.2 percent of single custodial fathers work less than full time
- 7 percent of single custodial mothers work more than forty-four hours weekly
- 24.5 percent of single custodial fathers work more that forty-four hours weekly
- 46.2 percent of single custodial mothers receive public assistance
- 20.8 percent of single custodial fathers receive public assistance[44]

Shockingly, 40 percent of mothers have reported that they disrupted visitation to punish the father, not caring about the impact this would have on the children.[45] For too many women, the focus after divorce is how they feel about their ex-husband, not what the children need from their father. Bitterness, anger, and vengeance are too often propped up by family courts, allowing a mother to exploit and punish her ex-husband just because she is a woman. These women will go to any lengths to keep the husband out of their lives, even falsely accusing him of abuse. Some justify disrupting their children's relationship with their father with claims that another man can fill his shoes. But this isn't the case. While having a good man in a child's life is better than none, and the many men who have adopted children are incredible role models and fathers for a child who doesn't have one, nothing can fully replace a loving biological father.

## BIOLOGY MATTERS, AND CHILDREN NEED THEIR BIOLOGICAL FATHERS.

My husband is one of the best stepfathers I've ever met. I know I might be biased, but I've talked to many divorced couples and, trying to be as objective as possible, I have rarely met a man who has been as good a male role model for my children as my husband. Intuitive, kind, and emotionally intelligent, he has navigated the many pitfalls of step-parenting with wisdom and grace. He has both loved my children and not tried to replace their father. He has never said anything negative about my children's dad, always stepping aside when they need their real father's support instead of rushing in to replace him.

Since my children lived with me most of the time, I had to resist the impulse to push my children into the arms of their stepdad. I wanted them to have a safe, loving relationship with him, but I knew he could not take the place of their father. This wasn't always easy to do—emotionally. It was difficult, at times, not to let my anger disrupt my children's relationship with their dad. I, unlike my husband, had a harder time not saying negative things about my ex-husband in front of the kids. When I did, I paid the price with my children's anger and distrust. Thankfully, my husband took his role as stepfather seriously—and wisely understood that his purpose was to support, not supplant or subvert. He never upstaged their father. He never told other people he was their dad, always making a point to say "stepdad," and he never considered asking them to call him Dad. That would be inappropriate.

The issue of calling a stepparent Mom or Dad is a point of conflict I've had when talking to other divorced parents. I strongly believe that, if the other parent is still in the picture—even remotely—it is disruptive to the children to call the stepparent mom or dad—even if the kids say it's okay. Children want to please adults and don't know what's best for them. It divides loyalty, is disrespectful to the other parent, and it's—let's be honest—not true. As a stepparent, you're not their parent, no matter how much you do for the child. You might have them 90 percent of the time, but that doesn't make you the biological mom or dad. You're the stepparent, and it's best for the children and overall family dynamics to act like it. No one said stepparenting is easy. You often have to give a lot without much in return. You take a lot of risks without a lot of benefits, but, if you do it right, love will grow between you and the children—a love that doesn't further disrupt their loyalties.

In our situation, the result of my husband doing it right has been a trusting and loving relationship between him and my children. But, even though my husband has been a solid presence in my children's lives, he is not their father. He will never be their father. I remember one evening when my son was in high school.

We were watching *Field of Dreams*, the baseball movie that tugs at the heart of every man and peels back the bandage of every male wound. In the film, Kevin Costner's character reconnects with his deceased father through baseball. I don't know many men who haven't been affected by the film. As I sat there with my son and his stepfather, I heard sniffles in the room. My son moved next to me, tears streaming down his face. My heart broke. I could see it in his eyes. He was missing his dad. I felt pangs of guilt over a divorce I caused. He loved his father, and even the love of the man in the room with him—a stepdad whose tears matched his own—could not soothe the ache of an absent father. I imagine my ex-husband shed many tears missing his son, tears I never saw but know in my heart were there.

This wasn't the only time my son cried for his father. I remember one day when he was taking karate lessons and he became frustrated and anxious because he wasn't performing the way he wanted. He dropped to his knees and wept, deep sobs coming from a place that had nothing to do with karate. His coach—a wonderful man and a great male role model—could not fill the emptiness in my son's heart. He needed the only man who could affirm him and validate him the way he needed. He needed his dad. Those tears were arrows in my soul, and I felt shame for causing that separation. I still feel it.

One of the greatest lies perpetrated on our society is that men don't care about being a parent. Women, it's assumed, are the ones who struggle to balance family and work, women strive to be the best parents, and women carry the burden of parenthood on their shoulders. This is not the case. According to the Pew Research Center, fathers are just as likely as moms to prioritize parenting. Fifty-seven percent of fathers say parenting is "extremely important to their identity," compared with 58 percent of mothers. They both see parenting as a positive in their lives, with 54 percent of fathers reporting that parenting is rewarding all the time, and 52 percent of moms reporting the same.[46]

Unfortunately, fathers seem to have a bit of an inferiority complex about their parenting abilities—thanks to a culture that continually tells them they're unworthy. Just 39 percent of dads feel like they do a good job raising their kids, compared with 51 percent of mothers. One issue that creates conflict is a difference in parenting styles. Sixty-four percent of parents believe moms and dads have their own way of parenting the kids, but they don't agree with why. Most men think it has to do with biology. Males and females differ, and this contributes to their unique approaches to parenting. Only about 30 percent of men believe these differences are rooted in social expectations. Women see things differently, which isn't surprising because one of the mantras of feminism is that masculinity and femininity are social constructs that can be changed through social engineering. The result is most mothers (66 percent) think the difference in parenting styles between men and women has to with society, not biology. While most people think these differences are good, too many elevate the role of the mom over that of the father.[47]

Obviously, from the testimony of human experience to statistics on fatherlessness, we know that fathers are integral to a family. This is true for both girls and boys. The first love in any girl's life is her father's. She learns from him her feminine value because her nature is highlighted against the background of his masculinity. He reveals her worth by protecting her in a way a mother can't. While a mother can go a long way protecting her children—beware of mama bears everywhere—nothing compares to the power of a man when he stands between a woman and danger. By witnessing masculine strength in the context of love, a girl develops a deep sense of security in herself and her place in the world.

## GIRLS NEED THEIR FATHER'S LOVE, AND THEY ARE DAMAGED WHEN THEY DON'T GET IT.

Intrinsic to being a man is protecting those he loves. A man's power, strength, emotional self-control, and aggression are not designed for mere self-expression. They serve a purpose—and that purpose is to love others and to do it fearlessly. "Don't be afraid," the prophet Nehemiah told the men who gathered before him. "Fight for your families, your sons and your daughters, your wives and your homes."[48] John Eldredge highlights this point in his book on masculinity *Wild at Heart*: "It's not just that a man needs a battle to fight; he needs someone to fight for."[49] His first battleground is in defense of his family. When a daughter feels the safety and protection of her father, she learns what a man's love looks like—and she will want that in her future relationships. She won't be afraid of a man's strength because she will know what its purpose is. She will also be able to discern when a man is abusing that strength because she will have seen it rightly exercised.

Girls who don't have their fathers or who have abusive fathers have a deep wound in their feminine soul that bleeds into all their relationships. While my father did so much good in my life, I have to be honest about how he treated me when I was young. I have often wondered throughout my life how my father's abuse affected me at the time, and why my mother's steadfast love didn't compensate for it. For one thing, when my father hit me or terrified me with his rage, I felt unprotected not only by him, but by my mother as well, though this was never her intent. She tried to make up for it in her own way, but I felt like it was a kind of abandonment of both—my father for doing it, and my mother for not stopping him.

I saw, from a young age, the misuse of male strength and the frailty of a woman in the face of it. Still, despite the abuse, I never lost the need of my father, longed for his protection, and looked for pinpricks of light to shine into the darkness of our relationship and heal some of the wounds. Over time, healing has come. I still suffer pangs from those wounds, as adult trauma has piled onto childhood fears. But the relationship has healed because I never reduced my father to the sum total of his sins—a lesson I learned well and have tried to exercise when personally dealing with people as an adult. I don't always succeed, but I try.

I have many memories of connecting with my father and closing the gap formed when I was very young, rebuilding broken bridges brought about by his own issues. I remember one such time in the early '70s when my family visited my dad's mom in Ohio. Bundled up in a scarf, gloves, and an oversized coat, I carefully made my way down the icy steps of my grandmother's row house. The air smelled of everything winter—the freshly falling snow and the aroma of pumpkin pie drifting from the open doorway, mixed with smoke from the fireplace. I was nine or ten and thrilled to see a white Christmas. We rarely had snow in North Carolina, so it was a treat to spend Christmas in Ohio with my father's relatives.

Bellaire was a small steel- and coal-mining town with steep hills that sloped down to the Ohio River. Across the river was Wheeling, West Virginia, and, at night, the factories lit up the sky, illuminating the tangled banks of the river and its dark, languid waters. Everything in Bellaire had a gray dullness to it from the ever-present soot billowing from heaters and stoves. We usually kept our shoes on in the house because if we didn't, our socks would be ruined. When I took a bath before going to bed, the water looked like a dirty puddle, and the bubbles had a dusky shade to them.

My grandmother's house didn't have a shower, just a large claw-foot tub with rust stains around the drain. The bathroom was dark, long, and narrow, with cold tile floors and a high ceiling. The house didn't have central heat, and the bathroom was freezing. The only source of heat was a cast-iron gas stove that lit up in a line of tiny blue flames that fascinated me. I used to get up out of the tub, dripping wet, and nestle as close as I could to the stove without getting burned, letting the hot flames dry my naked body.

As the snow sparkled and swirled in the silver light of the lamppost, my parents, my brother, and I waved to my grandmother as she stood on the porch, promising to have steaming city chicken for us when we got back from our stroll. City chicken is a misnomer. It doesn't actually have chicken in it. It was created when chicken was too expensive and all folks could buy was veal or pork. Resourceful people took pieces of pork and veal and wrapped it around a stick in the form of a drumstick and called it city chicken. I loved it, and I would eat it until my skinny belly was stuffed. I only had it when I went to Ohio, and, for me, it became synonymous with everything blue-collar and Northern.

I waved one last time to my grandmother as she stepped into the yellow glow of the house—the house where my father grew up as an only child, and where, when he was just six years old, he watched his father slowly die. For a year, my grandfather was confined to a bed with tuberculosis of the spine, unable to move. My dad took care of him, massaging his muscles when they tightened, listening to his stories and poetry he'd written. Evidently, my grandfather was an extraordinarily kind man, an artist at heart and a tender soul. My dad watched him die in the living room where they kept the bed, surrounded by remaining relatives who did not share my grandfather's gentle nature.

I wondered what that must have been like to experience such a loss at so young an age, and as I glanced over at my father walking hand-in-hand with my mother, I realized there was so much I didn't know about him, what he thought about, and what he felt. He was gone a lot when I was growing up, stationed overseas with the Marines, and then there was Vietnam. When he came home, it felt like a foreign invasion of our peaceful home. Quick-tempered and irritable, my dad seemed to be impatient with everything and everyone around him, particularly his scrawny, pale-eyed daughter who was often lost in daydreams and would step unknowingly on invisible tripwires that surrounded him. The backlash was immediate and painful, and I learned quickly to avoid him.

But that wasn't always possible. One day, I went roller-skating in our neighborhood. It was a bright blue summer day, and a boy I had a silly crush on lived near the highway at the entrance to the neighborhood. I decided to go up there and visit. On the way, I discovered that our dog had followed me. He was a little black terrier, full of life and spirit. I told him to go home, but he continued to follow. I thought about turning around and taking him back, but I wanted to see the boy up the road. So I just kept going, and my dog did too.

When I reached the house, several kids were already there playing in the driveway. I joined them, not paying attention to where my dog was. I hadn't been there long when I turned to find my bright-eyed dog standing in the middle of the road, panting happily. Terrified, I whistled for him to come. But he just stood there, staring at me. A truck was coming, and cars were already passing in the far lane. Horns blared. I wanted to run get him, but I couldn't; it was too dangerous with my roller skates on, so I got as close to the road as I could. "Come on, boy," I pleaded, clapping and whistling. "Come to me. Please, come!"

But it was too late. A truck barreled by, wind gusting over me, tires screeching, kids yelling, my dog's body lying on the road in a pool of blood. I heard myself scream, and I sunk to the ground, my knees slamming into the pavement. I don't know how long I stayed there, but someone had called my parents. The boy I had a crush on pulled me up and told me my dad was there. With tears streaming down my face, I half-stumbled, half-skated to the car, where my dad stepped from the driver's side, his face full of fury. Everything was a blur of fear and grief and tears. I hurried to him, holding out my arms for comfort. The next thing I knew, my head snapped back and pain shot through my cheek. He yelled for me to get in the car as he went and picked up my dog from the road.

The ride home was silent as I forced myself not to cry. I didn't want to make him even angrier. My chest burned from the effort. When we got home, my dad put my dog's body in a green military duffle bag and carried it to the back yard. I followed with my mom, but he told her to take me inside. He didn't want me there. He would bury the dog alone.

I watched my dad dig a hole from the living room window. After he was done, he came inside and went straight to the shower. He was in there a long time, and I could hear him, faintly, through the door, sobbing. I sunk to the floor outside the bathroom and listened to my father cry for the first time in my life. I wanted to comfort him, to tell him how sorry I was, to make it all right. But I knew I couldn't. I knew I couldn't make the pain go away, not any of it, but I wanted to—desperately—for his sake and mine.

Even as my cheek still burned from the back of his hand, I loved him. His tears betrayed his anger; it wasn't badness or cruelty that caused him to react the way he did, but pain and fear. I was young, just a child, but the mystifying complexities of life and of the human heart washed over me that day, infusing me with their deep realities, exposing me to the vulnerabilities of compassion, and leaving me both confused and consoled.

That Christmas Eve, as snow crunched beneath our feet along the river and memories of that day had faded into a dull ache, my dad shared stories of what it was like to grow up in a coal-mining town. How he and his friends sledded down the ice-covered streets, dodging traffic, until he crashed into a snowbank, nearly breaking an arm. How in the summer, he swam in the river and even saved a friend from drowning. How he was expected to work at the steel mill, living the same life everyone else had lived, but, after graduation, he joined the Marines instead. I listened, spellbound, as my father's world—for a moment—became mine.

The evening deepened and the wind off the water was turning icy. My stomach grumbled for city chicken. My face was frozen, and the gloves I wore were wet from snow. We turned back to head home, walking down a dimly lit street lined with old homes. The snow hid the usual dinginess of the town, with its rusting sheds, peeling paint, crumbling bricks, and cracked walkways. That night, everything was white—for just a little while before the soot turned the world gray once more. The air smelled clean and new. Christmas lights glittered on the snow as if rubies, emeralds, and sapphires had been spilled onto the street. A church bell sounded in the distance, filling the night like angels' voices.

It was getting colder, and I began to shiver. My dad looked down at me and pulled off my wet gloves. He held my frozen hands in his, rubbing them warm. Then he gave me his gloves and dusted snowflakes from my freckled nose. "Do you want me to carry you the rest of the way?" he asked. I nodded. He picked me up and, as fresh snow fell that Christmas Eve on the rundown homes that overlooked the river, on the uneven sidewalks and rusting fences, on the town with all its brokenness and imperfections, and on the imperfect man who held me in his arms, I tasted a moment of perfect peace—a moment I would carry with me for the rest of my life.[50]

## CHILDREN NEED TO BOND WITH THEIR FATHERS BY ENTERING THEIR FATHER'S WORLD.

Daughters, like sons, will always need their fathers, and they will look for ways to bridge any gaps to have that relationship. Sports were a great way for my dad and me to bond, either through my participating, his coaching, or us watching games together. That might sound more like a father-son bonding time, but it worked for me too. I was competitive and loved to play soccer and run track. My dad would take me to Camp Lejeune and make me run the long strip of highway toward the beach as he drove beside me, training me on hot summer days for cross country in the fall. He pushed me, and I loved him for it even though I hated how difficult it was in the moment. Sports were a part of his life as much as mine, and it was a delight to share athletic competition with him. It also made me appreciate and understand a man's love for developing skills and competing.

One of my favorite memories is snuggling on the couch on a cold winter Sunday in 1975 to watch the Super Bowl with my dad. I can still smell the freshly made popcorn that he popped in a copper kettle on the stove and drizzled with loads of melted butter. He placed the massive bowl between us, and we shared popcorn and Cokes as we watched the Pittsburgh Steelers, led by Terry Bradshaw and the Steel Curtain, beat the Vikings' Fran Tarkenton and the Purple People Eaters. To the sounds of munching popcorn, cheers of the crowd, the play-by-play of Curt Gowdy and commentary by Don Meredith, the bonds of a father-daughter relationship strengthened.

I loved to watch football. My mom was there too, lying back in her recliner, scratching my dog's ears; and my brother was spread out on the floor, crumbling Oreos into his vanilla ice cream before cookies and cream ice cream was a product on the freezer shelves at the grocery store. I loved the excitement of the game, the crushing tackles, the long throws, the sacks, the runs, and the last-second field goals that won the game. I didn't always understand what was happening. Sometimes I would ask, and my dad would patiently explain the difference between a field goal and an extra point, what a touchback meant, and why a team didn't go for it on every fourth down. Sometimes, when Dad's Steelers weren't doing very well, I'd keep my questions to myself and lick my buttery fingers. The details didn't matter anyway. It was enough to spend time with him, sharing a bowl of popcorn and being a part of his grown-up world that made me feel accepted and loved.

The most important man in a girl's life will always be her father. He has more influence on her than most any other person. He plays an integral role in the development of her self-image and self-esteem, her ability to cope with stressors, her understanding of relationships with men, and even her intellectual development. If you go to any parenting resource, you will find countless studies on the benefits of a father in a girl's life as well as advice on how to be a great dad. A common suggestion is for dads to spend time with their daughters—entering their world by doing what their daughters like to do, even if that means going to the mall or having a tea party with them, complete with My Little Ponies as guests.

I have to say that my dad never let me dress him in my princess costumes, and I don't think he ever played dolls or joined me for a tea party, but he did spend time with me. He coached my soccer team and attended every event I ever participated in—even dreadful middle school band concerts. If I was involved in something—whether it was shaking like a leaf while I performed a piano solo or running my heart out to make the North Carolina State Championship in track—my dad was there. I never had to scan the stands to find empty seats. There were my parents, camera in hand, watching me and cheering me on.

I had a friend in high school—a friend who never knew her dad—who told me one time in ninth grade that I was spoiled. "Spoiled!" I said. I was shocked. I was one of the least spoiled kids I knew. I grew up without much money, and my parents made me work for every dime I ever had. "No," she said. "Not *that* kind of spoiled. You're spoiled by your parents' attention.

They're always at your track meets and concerts. They never miss a soccer game. They're just always there. Especially your dad. You're spoiled with love."

I'll never forget her telling me that, and I realized at that moment how lucky I was. I felt a deep sadness for my friend, and I still do these many years later. Her dad left her and her mom when she was a baby. She never knew him. Her mom struggled. My friend was active in school, very accomplished, but she never had anyone to cheer her across the finish line at track meets or applaud her flute solos in band or when she won beauty contests. She felt the emptiness of her missing father, and it has haunted her throughout her life, a shadow darkening every relationship.

I never knew that pain, that loss. My father was present, and, while we didn't have tea parties or go shopping at the mall, and while I suffered under his heavy hand when I was younger, he did spend time with me—not just on my terms, but on his. He opened the door to his world and held my hand as I stepped through. One way he did that was through football. While it's good for fathers to get to know their daughters by engaging with them on their level—even if that means playing with Polly Pockets for an hour or so—that doesn't mean fathers *always* need to do what the daughter wants to do. Sometimes it's good, if not better, for the child to be brought into the father's sphere.

This doesn't mean that all lines between the adult and child should be erased. While it might sound outdated, the idea of a child knowing his or her place has some wisdom to it. It is good for children to learn respect for "adult space"—and especially male space—and realize that this is something they need to grow into through maturity. It's like a reward after much work, something they need to earn, not simply be given. Too many children run rampant over the home and adult gatherings, robbing parents of much-needed adult time and creating an atmosphere in which children think they are entitled to adult privileges. Allowing children to have this kind of free rein doesn't foster maturity—it fuels arrogance and disrespect. Adult women would do well to remember this when it comes to respecting a man's time and space. He's not being rude or inconsiderate if he doesn't devote every moment to his wife whenever she wants it. If he's watching a game, it's not toxic masculinity if he doesn't appreciate being interrupted when his wife just wants to chat.

That being said, for children there are times for them to come alongside their parents and be a part of their grown-up interests. The child might not always want to, but, if you start young enough, it will be easier. I don't remember my first football game and how I felt. As a girl, I'm sure I wasn't interested in the game in the beginning. The popcorn and Coke helped entice me, I'm sure. But I also liked being with my dad, doing something he enjoyed. It made me feel grown-up in a way and close to him. It also gave me the opportunity to learn the game itself—something I found beneficial as I got older.

Football isn't "just a game" to men. It touches part of their spirit as men—that inner "hunter" that gets little release in today's modern world. It allows them to bond with other men—the men on the field and the men they watch the game with. It develops a sense of loyalty you find on the battlefield, which is one reason they get so emotionally invested. Growing up watching football with my dad exposed me to the highs and lows of male competitive passion. This enabled me to understand it, not be intimidated by it, and even enjoy it when I became an adult.

Watching football with my dad has led to watching football with my husband. Some of the most relaxing times we have are sitting at on the couch or going to the sports bar, watching the Panthers trounce the Saints or the University of North Carolina destroy Duke. I have to confess, I still don't understand football the way my husband does. I think it helps to have played the game or been an avid follower to understand all the rules. I still ask questions (though I try to limit it to commercial time), but I have an uncanny ability to call disputed plays. My husband has learned not to argue with me when I insist a player caught the ball, fumbled, or broke the plane. I'm always right. He always rolls his eyes. (Seriously, I'm always right.)

When it comes to watching football with my dad, my husband has as much to be thankful for as I do. It's something we can share and enjoy. Instead of being a source of conflict, as it is with some couples, it's a time of joy. When he wants to watch a game, I don't feel threatened by it. It's something we can do together. I love to watch him get passionate about a score or even angry when someone makes a boneheaded play. It's a delight to hear him talk about "back in eighty-two," when he played. I can see the shadow of the little boy he once was—a time long ago when weekends were all about the game on Friday night, playing in the fields with friends on Saturday or, if it was raining, making paper footballs and flicking them across the table for hours, then watching the Cowboys on Sunday. Being able to share those memories with him and understanding just a hint of what he's feeling deepens our relationship—and I have my dad to thank for that.[51]

## BOYS NEED THEIR FATHERS TO TURN THEM INTO MEN.

While girls have their special bonds with their dads, boys have different relationship—one that truly defines not only their value, but their identity as men. Intrinsic to every man's life is the need to hear his father say, "You are my son and, in you, I am well pleased." Boys want to know that they're growing into men who will make their fathers proud. This doesn't make masculinity completely socially constructed. The fundamental elements of masculinity are rooted in a boy's nature by design. But, like the rational mind—a fundamental feature of humanity—it must be developed. We aren't born into a mature mind, and boys don't suddenly become masculine men. They must be properly trained, and most of that training is done by Mom getting out of the way and letting Dad do his job. Moms can't completely replace dads in this endeavor because femininity can never bestow masculinity—only masculinity can. Some men think that their masculinity is strengthened through the affirmation and validation of women. This is wrong. Men who think this way are not properly developed as men. They are still boys looking for Mom's approval. Men who have matured into their masculinity have had their manhood validated by other men—most importantly, by their father. To use an analogy, a football player doesn't measure his ability to play football by the praise of a ballerina. His skill is validated only by other football players, specifically older, better, and more competent experts at the game.

Boys are born with an intrinsic desire to go on an adventure. They feel energy, curiosity, and aggression coursing through them. "When boys play at war, they are rehearsing their part in a much bigger drama," Eldredge writes. "One day, you just might need that boy to defend you."[52] This is true even of the artists and scientists, the more intellectual and less physical boys. Physical strength isn't the only power a boy needs to develop. He needs to learn how to use his love of aesthetics, his creative mind, and mental prowess to serve his greater purpose as a man—to unlock the mysteries of life and to love others with a heart of service and sacrifice. Boys need to understand how they reflect the image of God the Father—the source of masculinity. They need to know and understand their power, both as males and unique individuals. They need to accept and feel comfortable with the reality that they are dangerous, but not always a threat—a description reminiscent of C. S. Lewis's depiction of Aslan, the lion in Narnia: "He isn't safe, but he's good."[53] Boys need to both express and respect their own strength but control it and use it wisely. Fathers are essential to showing their sons the path to manhood, and mothers are not equipped to do this. "Masculinity is an essence that is hard to articulate, but that a boy naturally craves as he craves food and water," Eldredge writes. "It is something passed between men.... Never receiving any sort of blessing from your father is a wound."[54]

We have a bittersweet running joke in our family that touches on this innate need of a son to have his father's approval. After my husband and his ex-wife divorced, decision-making about values instilled in the children were disrupted. My husband played football in high school and was a bit of a jock (though balanced with an intellectual/artist side). His ex-wife wasn't thrilled about sports and considered them too worldly. I don't know if she would put it in these terms exactly, but her view would come close to the idea that certain types of athletic competition breed toxic masculinity. Those views might have changed over time, but they were a part of the conflict between her and my husband when it came to raising their son. Regardless of the mother's values, my husband tried to get his son involved in sports, playing a little baseball and running track. But he was a late developer, and he didn't get the early training in sports that other boys had, so he was behind. Football, for instance, never came into the picture. This was a sore point at family gatherings when my husband's extended family would ask about my stepson's extracurricular activities. Being ardent football fans, they couldn't understand why he never played. Football was a family legacy of sorts. My stepson felt the disappointment every time the subject came up.

Despite reassurances from his father that it didn't matter whether he played football, my stepson couldn't shake the feeling that he had disappointed his dad. He hadn't proved his physical strength in a way that would be validated by his father. Again, my husband assured him that this wasn't the case, but it's something my stepson couldn't shake. Even though his dad said he was proud of him and validated him in many ways about his masculinity, this missing piece was like an itch he never could scratch. And so, what did he do? He became a U.S. Marine. He even joked as his 6'3" frame filled out with muscles and he towered over everyone around him, "Maybe now Dad will be proud of me." He says it with a grin, but it touches on a truth. This bothers my husband deeply, hating that his son would feel this need to prove his masculinity in such a dangerous way, but it's rooted in his nature. To be clear, my stepson has a lot of other reasons for joining the military. This is just a small part of it, and I don't think he feels like he needs to prove himself this way any longer—hopefully, the reassurances of his father have overcome those insecurities and healed those wounds. But they're still a little evident when my stepson inevitably challenges his dad to hot sauce-eating contests, reducing my husband to tears and the rest of us to laughter. Like other men, this instinctual need is integral to his nature as a man, and it can't be denied. Boys need their father's validation as men.

This need to develop manliness is the whole point of male initiation. Women get their periods, but in most cultures, men have had to be initiated into manhood by spilling blood another way—either literally or figuratively. The initiation rites vary in a thousand different ways from culture to culture, but all focus on one thing: a boy must do something to prove he is a man. His masculinity is active, and he must be approved by his father and the men in his culture to be a man. Those who seek to "reconstruct" masculinity oppose this overt male initiation, claiming it breeds toxic masculinity and makes men have to prove something they shouldn't—and makes those who can't feel badly about themselves.

Removing this social pressure from boys is one of the goals of pro-feminists, as they claim that this pressure from other males causes men to be depressed, discontent, and even suicidal. They think it is enough that men emotionally support their sons, be present in their lives, and love them with authentic attachment. While it is true that boys need their fathers to be present, they don't need second mothers. They need their father—and anyone who has seen a boy's eyes light up when his father praises him, puts his hand on his back in affirmation, or gives him a thumbs up when he cracked a baseball over a fence knows what I'm talking about. A father's pride fills a son's soul. Men are depressed because they didn't get enough of this, not because they were pressured to attain it.

Feminized psychology tries to protect men and boys from the judgment of others and from the anxiety of developing into men. Pro-feminists insist that men can passively become manly, expressing their masculinity merely by being males. If their particular "masculinity" is acting like a woman, for instance, then so be it. His manliness, they claim, is relative to himself, even if it's feminine. This leads pro-feminist psychologists to claim that there can be as many different kinds of masculinity as there are men on the planet. But this conflates masculinity and individuality. It's true that how men express their masculinity according to their personalities, abilities, and pathologies is as varied as men themselves. But masculinity is still a commonality among all males, just as their humanity is.

While there are billions of human beings on this planet that are each unique, they all share common elements of being human. Rationality, morality, physical form, ability to love and self-reflect—these are all human traits shared by all humans, though each expresses them differently. Likewise, masculinity is universal while also being particular. Strength, aggression, and minds that are physically constructed differently than a woman's are all universal, but so is the active nature of masculinity. "A man's effectiveness is measured as others see him in action," David Gilmore writes, "where they can evaluate his performance.... It means decisive action that works or serves a purpose, action that meets tests and solves real problems consensually perceived as important."[55] Who better than the father who knows his son—both as an individual and as a male—to initiate him into manhood?

We have raised too many boys in a feminized environment without the will or desire to do the hard work of manliness. Our subjective and sensitive age with its luxury of technology has created a soft identity for men so that they are both bored and frustrated at the same time. They have been stranded among women, softened by their approval, and emotionally weakened so that, when they're told to "Man up," they resent it. Men are emotionally dependent today on women, not because they want to share their emotions with women, but because they seek validation for who they are as men from women. They have been wounded by the absence of their fathers and their need to be developed into men by those who have walked the path before them.

The best thing mothers can do is get out of the way so fathers can raise their sons to be men. Part of that instruction is a father teaching his son how to be a truly free human being, not to do whatever he wants for any material gain, but to use his freedom to love others. Boys want their fathers to look at them and say, "Well done, son." They want their fathers to encourage them, motivate them, and help them reach deep within and bring all that is good and noble to the surface. Good fathers see what's inside their sons—character and abilities—and know how to teach their sons to be the best they can be. Basketball coach Jim Valvano once said that his father gave him the greatest gift anyone could give another person—"he believed in me." Men need to be believed in, and that belief begins with their fathers. It continues with the women who love them.

CHAPTER 6

# MEN AS WARRIORS (WOMEN AREN'T SUPERHEROES)

*My body is strong, my mind is sound, my soul is fierce, yet quiet. I am slow to anger and swift to action. I am just, and I countenance no evil.*

—The Good Man Project

I stared down the field with sweat rolling into my eyes. I wiped my face and prepared to run. It was the all-girls soccer championship, and the score was zero to zero. Only two minutes were left in the game, and I didn't want to face a grueling round of penalty kicks. We were determined to beat the one team that had challenged us all year for the number-one spot.

The game was a vicious middle-school rivalry, complete with cursing, hair-pulling, jabbing elbows, and an occasional punch when the referee wasn't looking. As captain, I was one of the primary targets. I'd also racked up more goals against this team than anyone else all season. The goalie was out for blood, as was the massive center defender who could have passed for a linebacker on the high school football team.

The summer sun beat down on us from a hard, blue sky. The grass had turned brown, and bare patches spotted the field. The air smelled of pine and dirt and body odor. After a long game in ninety-eight-degree heat, I was covered in grime; blood dripped down my leg from a defender's cleat. I was exhausted, but I wasn't about to give up. When I saw an opening, I took it. I raced down the sideline past the midfielders then cut to the center of the field, motioning for a teammate to pass the ball. She kicked it right to my feet. I trapped it and turned only to find myself face-to-face with the dreaded defender. I faked to the right then dribbled around her to the left. I can still hear her blood-curdling scream in my ears. She might have been big, but she was slow.

The only player between the net and me was the goalie. She squared off, and I shot the ball, hard and straight. It slammed into her face, and she hit the ground. Luckily, it bounced right back to me. With the goalie down, I took a single step and tapped the ball gently into the corner of the net. The ease with which I did it was an added insult. Five seconds later, the game was over.

The goalie jumped up and ran toward me, yelling, "You're going to pay for that!" Like a typical girl, she took the loss personally. The foul language that followed was mercifully drowned out by the celebration on the sidelines. I ignored her as I joined my teammates to receive our trophies, but I could see a gang forming on the far side of the field—soccer players, boyfriends, thugs from the city high school. They were milling about, glancing in my direction. I knew I wouldn't be able to avoid them on my way to the parking lot. I thought about asking some of my teammates for help, but I didn't. I don't know why. Pride maybe. More than likely, I didn't think they'd be much help against the mob. I looked for my coach, but he was busy talking to a group of parents. So I procrastinated, gathering up my gear. By the time I was done, most of my teammates were gone.

Taking a deep breath and bracing myself for a confrontation, I headed toward the parking lot. But as I reached the far end of the field, I noticed my dad was waiting for me. Usually, I met my parents at the car after a game, but he waved me over. "Keep close," he said in that gruff, no-nonsense Marine Corps voice that usually terrified me. I walked next to him right through the pack with their glares and muttered threats. When we reached the car, I let myself breathe.

"You didn't have to do that, Dad," I said. He looked at me, and I knew he could see right through my feeble attempt at bravery.

"Yes, I did." At that moment, my dad was my hero, my knight in shining armor, and I've never forgotten it. That day had such a profound impact on me because I wasn't raised to be a damsel in distress, a princess in a tower to be rescued. It was the '70s, after all, and society was high on the drug of egalitarianism. My dad was in full support and raised me as if I were a boy. Whining was forbidden. Weakness wasn't tolerated. He'd tell me to stop crying and get back on my bike after I fell and skinned my knee. He'd toss me into the deep end of the pool and tell me to sink or swim. He'd make me go out and mow the lawn just as my brother did and clip the hedges with hand-clippers until they were perfectly even (I can still feel the blisters). When my dad caught me picking a fight after getting off the school bus, he didn't reprimand me or tell me I wasn't acting ladylike. Instead, he said if it ever happened again, I needed to come home first and change out of my school clothes before bloodying them up—and, if I did pick another fight, then I'd better be sure I could win.

He was determined to toughen me up, at least when I needed to be. So, when my dad came to my rescue after the soccer game, it meant something significant. It meant he saw that I truly needed him, that I was scared, and that it was his job, not just as my father but as a man, to protect me. I didn't resent it for a moment. I loved it. It filled my heart like nothing else. I longed for his protection, and I still crave that masculine strength—from my husband and in a broader sociological sense from all men for all women.

Modern-day feminism claims that chivalry is chauvinism in disguise, that It's a patriarchal assumption that women are weak, that they can't get by in life without the help of a man, and that anytime a man helps a woman, he's treating her as a subordinate. When a man opens a door for a woman, too many feminists assume he couldn't possibly be doing it out of respect; instead, he's stroking his ego, treating her as if she's helpless without him. Nothing could be further from the truth.[56]

## WHEN MEN ARE STRONG, BOTH MEN AND WOMEN BENEFIT.

Not long ago, I went to the store to buy firewood. I lifted two mesh bags and lumbered outside into the sprinkling rain, trying to keep them from dragging on the wet ground. As I walked to the parking lot, a man hurried over and asked if he could help. I nodded, handing him a bag. He graciously took both. "I'm sure you can do this yourself," he said, "but I just—"

I interrupted him with a wave of my hand, "Yes, I can, but you made it so I don't have to. Thank you." He smiled, obviously relieved that he wouldn't be accused of overstepping his bounds. I was just thankful to be relieved of the heavy load.

The issue wasn't my capability. I could make it to the car, but I certainly couldn't have done it as easily as the gentleman who volunteered to help. He saw me laboring and offered his hand. Instead of letting pride rule me, I humbly let him take the bags. His offer of service lifted both of our spirits. It gave him the satisfaction of doing his manly duty to help a woman—men love to serve women when they know it's appreciated. And it gave me relief from muscle strain. It also made me grateful. I didn't know the man, but, in that brief moment, a little bit of trust and appreciation were forged in the world of men and women.

To the modern feminist, however, such chivalry is about male domination, not virtue. "Women don't need men!" they often claim. Such thinking is based on a falsehood. Women can certainly be strong. They can and should have equal opportunities. They can compete in many areas and even stand up for themselves when they need to, but this doesn't mean women don't need men. Women are the softer sex. They need a man's physical strength, his emotional fortitude, his focused way of looking at life, and his masculine wisdom.

To have this need doesn't mean women are subordinates. It means they are incomplete *in human relations*. It means they don't need to go it alone. They can try. They might even succeed in some form or another, but at what cost? Is the isolating independence worth it? What have women sacrificed by denying their nature and denying men theirs? In truth, women have sacrificed something very fundamental—the peace, contentment, and wholeness that come when we each live according to our created natures, natures that are interdependent and complete only when we meet the needs of the other. We aren't designed to go it alone. We are designed to be helpmates.

One reason people are so lonely today is we have abandoned our need for one another. We live with a hyperindividualistic mindset in which autonomy is valued over community. As a lover of political liberty, I don't want to exchange individualism for collectivism. That's not the kind of community I'm talking about. I'm referring to the nature of people as social creatures. We are not meant to live in isolation. This is especially true of the relationship between men and women, not just as husbands and wives, but as fellow sojourners along the path of life. Human beings are primarily relational, and we relate to one another in a variety of ways. Our sexuality is a basis for one type of relating, and the differences between men and women create a need for completion—for company as we go through life.

Modern feminism fills women with holes, and one of the biggest is that they can exist without men. They're told that men and women are the same, perfectly equal, and they don't really need male support. But they do. They are different from men, and therein exists their need. Women turning their backs on the men in their lives leaves them wanting. The power feminism promises is an illusion. The sexual revolution that was supposed to make women equal with men has made them victims of their own choices. Women have deprived themselves of the security that a man loves them for who they are, not for what they can give him. Women have given up their power to make men prove to them they are worthy suitors as they easily give away their bodies for sex without accountability. Women have cheapened themselves. They have exchanged their femininity for a delusional equality, and they are lesser for of it.

In marginalizing the importance of men in a woman's life, feminism has violently corrupted the feminine soul. Women's spirits are sick with pride, and none of the typical things they look to fill their lives will heal it. Not casual sex. Not money. Not a career. Not a reconstructed "family" with no husband or father. Not carrying their own bags and fighting their own battles. Only humility can save them. Now, more than ever, women need men—strong, virtuous men—to lift them when they've fallen, to bind them up when they're broken, and to protect them when they're threatened by other people, by natural disasters, by the toils and struggles of life, and by powerful institutions that seek to rob us all of our liberty. Women need to let men be men. Only in mending this severed relationship can our society be healed.

I wonder, as I think back on that day so long ago and how my father's strength made me feel loved and valuable, whether we can overcome years of anger and bitterness to find that place where a woman is willing to depend on a man, to reach out her hand for him to take, to hold, to kiss, and to protect. I believe we can, but it won't happen if women point their fingers at men and tell them they're the problem. Women need to look in the mirror and see how they've failed to appreciate men as the warriors who fight on their behalf. Instead of "leaning in" and constantly proving themselves, women need to be willing to lean on men. That takes trust.

When it comes to the issue of men being aggressive, competitive, and protective, men have a lot to say to women:

"Women need men to be strong if they want to keep their freedom."

"Stop trying to turn me into a girly man."

"Female superheroes aren't real, so stop pretending."

"I don't want a woman in combat because I don't want to lose the masculine virtue of needing to protect her."

"Technology is a great equalizer between men and women, but sometimes there's no technology around to save you—only a man."

"I'm willing to take the bullets for others, but it makes it a lot harder when women don't respect your sacrifices."

"Civilization was built by man's strength, not women's. Women contributed in other necessary ways, but it was the aggression of men—forging through the unknown, fighting and dying in wars, and doing all the physical hard work it takes to build societies—that has made the world what it is today."

"If you think you're physically equal to men, then you should be required to sign up for selective service and fight right along the men on the front lines."

## MASCULINITY IS DANGEROUS, BUT IT IS ALSO GOOD.

The notion that men are a threat to women and predatorily aggressive has pitted women against men in just about every area of life. It has eroded trust. It has fostered feminist propaganda that men are guilty until proven innocent. In his book *Masculinity Reconstructed: Changing the Rules of Manhood*, Ronald Levant wrongly equates undeveloped masculinity and bad character with "traditional masculinity." When it comes to strength and aggression, he writes, "Meeting every act of aggression with an even greater display of aggression" is a "traditional masculine ethic." An example of this, Levant continues, "is that a man should show force when another man takes his parking place."[57] In the context of masculinity in America, this is simply nonsensical. Inherent in traditional masculinity has been the virtue of self-control. Historically, men who were unable to master their anger and their desires paid the price in society. They weren't trusted as "real men."

A newspaper account from 1769 in North Carolina tells a story about a man who was physically abusive to a woman, entering her house uninvited, and breaking down the door. She responded by grabbing a gun and shooting his arm off. The newspaper account offered no justification for the man's aggressive behavior. Instead, the reporter said that the man fell "victim to female vengeance, *which he had justly provoked.*" This kind of commentary on men without self-control was common. As Thomas Foster writes in *Sex and the Eighteenth-Century Man*, men like this "served as a symbol of the loss of masculine honor and self-control."[58] American men, who were raised in the Christian ethic or deeply affected by it, were taught that to be a man was to be circumspect and to exercise self-restraint. "Be watchful, stand firm in the faith," Paul wrote in his first letter to the Corinthians, "act like men, be strong. Let all that you do be done in love."[59] This is the core of traditional masculinity, and it was predominant in most of American history. It has been with the rise of feminism that these restraints have been loosened—both for men and women. Today, immorality and lack of self-control exist too often with impunity—a result of the sexual revolution, not traditional masculinity.

## Men need to be taught self-control; they don't need to be reconstructed through social engineering.

Instead of challenging men to be fully developed in their masculinity, pro-feminist psychologists are redefining traditional masculinity according to those who aren't masculine (women and emasculated males) and then pushing men to change, to become less masculine. This push to reconstruct masculinity is based on a false premise that there is something inherently wrong with male aggression—that it's emotionally unaware. This error is glaring in Levant's statement that "men possess a host of admirable skills and traits—but emotional intelligence isn't one of them." He goes on to say that our grandfathers and great-grandfathers "weren't too emotionally inclined," adding

> Too much emotional awareness and sensitivity would only have compromised their ability to do the things a man had to do: withstand long hours of backbreaking, sometimes dangerous work in the fields, mines, and factories to provide food and shelter for their dependants; be prepared at all times to lay their lives on the line to rescue families from danger and protect them from harm; leave their loved ones behind to seek work in distant locales when there was none to be found near home; go off to war—never knowing when or if they'd return—to maim and kill, or be maimed and killed by, other human beings.[60]

This need for "stoicism" is all well and good, Levant says, but times have changed, and we don't live like this any longer. Men don't need this emotional distance, strength, and aggression because they are living and working in a softer environment—and living softer means men need to become softer, he asserts. They need to be more sensitive and respect other people's feelings and become "more emotionally intelligent human beings." Levant argues that this requires men to throw off their traditional masculine values by figuring out "the ways in which their adherence to traditional values prevents them from doing that, then decide how best to reconstruct these aspects of their masculine code."[61]

Why and how did things change? The answer is complex, but one big piece of the puzzle is women changed their roles. They became equal providers and no longer wanted to focus their emotional energy on sustaining relationships. Levant says that in the past, men worked to make money, and women worked on relationships. Men haven't changed much—to the chagrin of people like Levant—though I do think that, even in the past, men worked on relationships, just in a different way. They kept the family together and moving forward in the practicalities of life—a relational endeavor—while women focused on feelings and personal interactions. But today, after decades of feminist hyperindividualism, women aren't as willing to do their part as they once did. They're just too busy. Because they're not dependent on men for economic support, Levant says, "Women today are also no longer so willing to do all the relationship work. 'Look, if you care about this relationship, [women tell men] you're going to have to work at it too.'"[62]

The goal, Levant claims, is for men to stop being *active* with their empathy and develop *emotional* empathy. In other words, they need to learn to share and express their feelings because the woman isn't doing it any longer—or, if she is, she needs the man in her life to do it too. Levant gives men some practical advice on how to develop this emotional empathy—advice that seems rather contrived. He tells them to develop a new vocabulary of emotions, such as "hurt," "sad," "disappointed," and "afraid." He advises them to study how actors and actresses communicate emotions by watching how they "use tone of voice, phrasing, facial expression, physical gestures, and body posture to express feeling," and then "apply what you've learned from watching make-believe to real life."[63] In other words, look to fiction not just as analogy, but to develop a new reality. If anything sums up the mindset of feminism, it's that.

Levant's observations that communication is suffering in relationships today are quite true, but his solutions erode masculinity and thereby cause men to feel disconnected from their core identity. The same thing has happened to women. They've eroded their femininity, and they are disconnected from who they really are—something that has left them feeling out of sorts in this new feminized world. This disturbance within the feminine psyche explains why women are starting to rethink their choices, and many are returning home to raise children. Technology has not only made it easier for women to stay and work from home, but they want to do it because they are happier raising children and putting their families first.

The vision of the feminist professional panacea turned out to be a mirage. Should men be forced down the same road only to find the same discontent at the end of it? Of course not. Yet this is what's happening in the demand for masculine reconstruction. Being open to some change and willing to work on communication is one thing—life isn't stagnant. But reconstruction of identity is another. Men who are trying to pick up the emotional slack and take on a more feminine tone might be communicating better with their wives and girlfriends, but they feel unsettled in themselves. They've traded something essential to their identity—that active empathy—for a pragmatic fix to a problem women and technology created.

Pro-feminists like Levant push for this change of identity by labeling men in negative tones, such as accusing them of being emotionally unintelligent. This is bizarre and has more to do with personality than sex. The most emotionally intelligent people I know are men—my husband being one of them—and some of the most emotionally stupid people I know are women. Maybe what Levant really means is emotionally expressive, but this is not the same thing as emotionally intelligent. By putting it in this frame, men are made out to be the problem and told they must become "smarter" to deal with the changes women have made in society. This negativity frustrates men, and rightly so.

## Stop trying to make men emote like women.

Even though women are working more, the core sexual nature of men and women hasn't changed. This is the fundamental issue our society doesn't want to face. The intransigence of nature is an obstacle we keep bashing our heads against, and it has frustrated us. Women will always be more emotionally expressive than men because that is part of their makeup as women. To change it would be damaging to the feminine psyche. One has to ask the obvious question: if times have changed because women have changed their roles, then why is it that men—whose roles have not been fundamentally altered, even with women in the workplace—must change who they are to accommodate women? Why don't women complete the "transition" and change who they essentially are and become less emotionally needy and express more active empathy? Why don't women learn to be satisfied with getting things done in the home rather than sharing their emotions and expecting men to take up the emotional slack? Why not have women become more like men rather than demanding that men become more like women? Why don't women watch actors and actresses in action movies and learn to apply emotional self-control to their real lives? A little *John Wick* might go a long way in building mutual understanding. No woman I know would agree that this is healthy, even those who love *John Wick* as I do. Yet women think it is perfectly acceptable to force men to reconstruct their masculinity to bring balance to the sexual energies that have been supposedly lost by women entering the workplace.

The assumption behind the pro-feminist's call for masculine reconstruction is that femininity—through feminism—has already been reconstructed to become more masculine, leaving a lack of balance in relationships—and, on the surface, it has, but it's only on the surface. The hope of pro-feminists is that through reconstructing sexuality, men and women will meet somewhere in the androgynous middle. But it's not working. That's because men are still expected to continue to be the men they've always been as providers and protectors—even as women deny they want this—while they're told to change to be like women. This is a big part of the mixed messages that confuse men today. Women imagine they've become more masculine because of the roles they fill, but they haven't changed that much ontologically. They're still women. They still express as women. They still have emotional needs as women. They still have emotional empathy, no matter how the roles change—because it's their nature.

The problem we're facing in our society is we are forcing both men and women to be something they're not and silencing them when they express those differences. The feminist experiment is failing, and this is reflected in the high levels of unhappiness and loneliness experienced by both men and women. Restructuring the masculine and feminine isn't working, but men are getting all the blame and told they must be something they're not to accommodate women who claim they've changed, when they actually haven't. You can say a woman needs a man like a fish needs a bicycle all you want, but the fact is the fish is still a fish, and a man isn't a bicycle. He's the water. And fish need water.

## The idea that women have become "equal" to men isn't as true as feminists assume.

Levant argues that the need for manly traits is disappearing because we live in a cushy society. He assumes that men will just be happier if they give up and act like women to fill the space left by technology and women who no longer want to carry the emotional burdens of working on intimate relationships. How wrong he is, despite his cited evidence that men who do what he advises are happier. They might be in the short-term, and some individual situations might be improved with better communication skills, but the societal push for widespread masculine reconstruction is having deleterious effects on the male psyche—and it's not because men aren't doing enough to become feminized. There is something deeper at work in the human condition that secular psychologists are ignoring, and men are feeling it. They're frustrated by it. Women might be working more in a competitive workplace, but men are still working alongside them. Men still provide for their families. Men still go to war and serve in combat. Men still do most of the dangerous jobs in our society, protecting women from harm. Men still step into the line of fire when a gunman opens on a crowded room. A young man exemplified this as he tackled a shooter at the University of North Carolina at Charlotte. Because of his sacrifice, his classmates were saved. His masculine instinct drove him to protect others, even if it cost him his life—and it did. Women aren't driven by these instincts, except when it involves children.

Men still have to find the strength to press on in their jobs, while women often leave their careers. They continue working while women take off to raise their children or to be with their families. I watched a cooking competition recently in which one of the female contestants quit the show because she wanted to be with her family. The show's hosts were disappointed, but they didn't criticize her. While you never like to see a person quit, a woman doing it took the edge off. I've never seen a man quit a competition to be with his family (unless there was an emergency). And, let's be honest—if he did, he wouldn't be held in as high esteem as the woman.

Some might think this is why masculinity should be reconstructed, that men should be able to quit a competition or work to go home just like a woman can—without judgment. That sounds like a pretty egalitarian ideal, but it's not realistic. Men are hardwired by God and nature to be strong, to protect, to work hard, and to kill the bad guys. This hasn't changed, no matter how many women flood the workplace or how technology changes our lives from hardship to ease. Life is turbulent. We have a deep sense, as human beings, that circumstances can change in an instant. Leisure can disappear in the blink of an eye, and we want to be assured—deep down—that we have what it takes to survive.

This anxiety is why dystopian literature and films are so popular. It's why series like *The Walking Dead* captivate us—we want to know that when technology falls apart and women are forced to face their natural weaknesses, there are strong men like Rick Grimes who will sacrifice their lives to save civilization. There is a beacon of reality within each of us that a time could come when we will need men to be men. It's a funny thing that feminism plays with this instinct by infusing powerful women into these fictional tales of desolation. It accounts for the preponderance of female action heroes. But, even in this, we know in our hearts that it's a myth. Reality always betrays the fantasies we create for ourselves.

One of the fantasies too many cling to is the idea that we don't live in a dangerous world. Yet terrorist attacks continue. Wars wage in foreign lands that threaten to involve the United States. The global society is smaller now, so conflicts abroad can more quickly become crises at home. The rise of militant Islam has replaced the Soviet Union as America's number-one menace, though Russia and China are still creeping around the edges, potential threats that could end our life of ease with the firing of a nuclear weapon into the heart of America.

We need strong men now as much as ever. We know the benefit of their strength from past wars. My grandfather—a member of the Greatest Generation—fought in World War II. I still remember, as a young girl, sitting wide-eyed when he would tell of battles he fought and deaths he witnessed. He was a Marine at the first landing at Guadalcanal, the Allies' first major offensive in the Pacific and a turning point in their favor. He would begin to describe the bodies of Japanese soldiers that stacked up along the coast, but his voice would trail off—only the faraway look in his eyes told of the horrors he witnessed. The Japanese lost twenty-four thousand men in that battle, compared with sixteen hundred on the American side.

The brutality of it haunted my grandfather and he was never the same. He, and other men like him through battles and wars across the centuries of human history, carried that burden so women don't have to. My grandfather was a stern man, but as someone who lived through the Depression and fought in a horrific war, he needed to be. Such was his sacrifice. Such was his duty as a man.

Not all men who've been in war show such reserve. I recently spoke to an old friend of my family about his tour in Vietnam. He was badly injured, having his legs ripped to shreds in battle. It took months to recuperate, and he almost died. He spoke to me not of the fighting, but of what it was like to come home to a country that disrespected his sacrifice—the pain it caused, the resentment it fueled, and the reaction it created as men asked to return to the battlefield to avoid hatred at home. As he told me his story, tears welled up in his eyes. "Whenever vets meet, we greet each other with a phrase that captures everything about that time," he said. "We say, 'welcome home,' because no one else would say it." How many men feel this lack of appreciation, even hostility, in the face of sacrifices they make—even if it doesn't involve war? How many simply want to be appreciated—to be welcomed home?

## A MAN'S VULNERABILITY IS VERY REAL; IT JUST DOESN'T LOOK LIKE A WOMAN'S.

The need for masculine strength doesn't always translate into the emotional absence pro-feminists often accuse men of exhibiting. Self-control and stoicism are not the same things. Men feel deeply, some more than others. They can be emotionally hurt, depressed, frustrated, sad, and full of joy. They're vulnerable, just not in the same way as women—and this is by design. Yet pro-feminists claim there's a crisis in the world of men because they're not vulnerable, once again painting men as the problem because they supposedly won't make emotional connections that put them at risk. Speaking as a woman, I don't like to be vulnerable either, but we're used to it because we're weaker by nature. Men, however, are not as fragile, and, unless you're going to weaken them with feminine hormones, they're always going to be less vulnerable physically. This, however, doesn't mean they're not emotionally at risk. To take the hits, to restrain yourself, to love deeply is to open yourself up to pain. It takes strength to love in the face of that insecurity. This is especially true for a man who is ready and willing not only to lay down his heart for a woman, but his life. "To love at all is to be vulnerable," C. S. Lewis writes.

> Love anything, and your heart will certainly be wrung and possibly broken. If you want to make sure of keeping it intact, you must give your heart to no one, not even to an animal. Wrap it carefully round with hobbies and little luxuries; avoid all entanglements; lock it up safe in the casket or coffin of your selfishness. But in that casket—safe, dark, motionless, airless—it will change. It will not be broken; it will become unbreakable, impenetrable, irredeemable.[64]

In the megahit TV series *Game of Thrones*, the character Grey Worm is a soldier who had been programmed not to feel anything—only to fight. He's the ultimate warrior who could be bought and sold to fight for anyone. All of the Unsullied, as they're called, were trained through brutal brainwashing (they had to kill babies in front of their mothers until they didn't feel anything). All love and fear of loss were driven from their hearts. Grey Worm was the best warrior among the Unsullied until he met Missandei, a beautiful woman who fell in love with him. He resisted, but over time, he fell in love with her. When that happened, he suddenly found himself feeling something he had never felt before—vulnerability. "You are my weakness," he told her. "When Unsullied are young, the masters learn their fears, but I had no fears. I was never the biggest, never the strongest, but I was the bravest, always. Until I met Missandei from the Isle of Naath. Now I have fear."[65]

If your boyfriend or husband loves you, he is vulnerable. His heart is not in a bunker protected from harm. It's alive and willing to do anything for you. Just because he doesn't share his emotions like a woman doesn't mean he isn't feeling them. Give him time and the right moments, and he will share them—because he trusts you. Listen to the emotions behind the words even if he doesn't say them. This is one of the differences between men and women when they communicate. Men stick to the facts, but they're filled with emotion. Women express their feelings, even when they don't conform to the facts. To demand that men become emotionally expressive just like women merely because women are busy in the workplace and emotionally exhausted, often unhappy, and frustrated by not being able "to do it all," doesn't mean women should make men just as uncomfortable by forcing them to be something they're not.

## Enough with the men's touchy share groups.

A new trend is on the rise in our culture to encourage men to sit around in groups and share their emotions with other men. It's different from those in the past—the beating of drums around campfires popular in the '70s. Now men are told they need to be physically and emotionally present with other men, touching one another to learn intimacy without feeling sexual. This scheme is a big part of the American Psychological Association's reconstruction of masculinity in its quest to drive what it calls "homophobia" from traditional men. When I mention this to my male associates, most shiver—and it's not because they're homophobic. It's because they're masculine men wired to connect this way with women, not with men. Most masculine men don't need to artificially share their deepest feelings with other men—or sit around cuddling each other. This aversion to male intimacy doesn't mean they don't share their feelings or even have physical contact. I know plenty of men, especially in churches, who gather together to share and keep one another accountable. Plenty of men's movements have emphasized the need to meet with other men but, even in this, it's not often the way women do it. The deep waters of a man's heart are not easily broken to gush forth for all to see—and this isn't a bad thing. It makes the bond between a husband and a wife even more special because he shares his heart and his body only with her. And it honors the emotional self-restraint men need to experience stability in their lives and to be comfortable in their own skin as men.

Pro-feminists would disagree, accusing men who only want to share their deepest feelings with their wives or girlfriends of being too "female dependent" in the expression of their feelings. This can be true for some men—those who can't connect with other men on any level because they have mommy issues. But a man who chooses to spill his guts only to his wife is a man who cherishes the intimacy of a trusted relationship and understands the wholeness of the man and woman in marriage. They long for that connection. I sometimes wonder if the increase of men's groups to share their feelings is due to women no longer being emotionally present with men in a way men need them to be. Women who demand that men always emotionally connect *as they do* often fail to emotionally connect with men in a way that brings comfort to the man.

When a man chooses a woman to love and adore for the rest of his life, he gives himself to her fully. She—not a bunch of men in a yoga class—is the other half of his heart. He doesn't verbally share it as often as the woman, but he's connected to her in the things he does. He wants her close, as long as she is letting him be himself. She is made for him to soothe his mind and chase away the specters of loneliness. God made Eve for Adam so he would not be alone. He didn't make Adam a group of dudes to hang with for emotional support. This doesn't mean men don't need other men; they do, but the kind of intimacy pro-feminists are demanding from men to be shared with other men should be reserved for that covenantal relationship in which trust, unity, and intimacy have been nurtured.

## A man is made in God's image—not a woman's.

Reconstructing masculinity into an emotionally expressive state is to ignore the real need for a man to be physically strong and aggressive when he needs to be. Just as Levant admitted, there's a reason men are emotionally reserved. They have hard jobs to do that don't provide the luxury of emotional expression. Even if they're not actively doing those jobs, it's still their nature. They keep those feelings inside so they can perform. Hard times require a man to be hardened for the tasks, and—let's face it—for most of human history, times have been hard. Survival has been imperative, and strong, competent men are necessary for that survival. Masculinity is universal because men are designed by God for specific purposes—that's true whether we're in a state of survival or not.

When you look at all the cultures that have ever existed, it's not an accident that one of the universal qualities of masculinity is protector—the archetypical warrior. In *Manhood in the Making*, David Gilmore examined cultures throughout history and found that, "regardless of other normative distinctions made, all societies distinguish between male and female, all societies also provide institutionalized sex-appropriate roles for adult men and women." Under all the surface differences among cultures is a "common ideal" of masculinity. This striving for manhood, for development of strength, emotional self-control, and competence is "not just in warrior cultures, but in peaceful ones too."[66] Gilmore is not ready to agree that there is a "universal male" as author Thomas Gregor concluded in his works and as I assert, but his research supports it. How masculine strength is developed varies very much from culture to culture, but the value of masculine power does not.

Essential to this strength is, as I've said, emotional self-control. The more a man becomes an emotional sieve, the less effective he will be when aggression is required. The more a man becomes like a woman, the less he will be able to be a man. Men and women are different. Men have feelings just like women, but they express them very differently—that expression is tied to their masculine power. Have a man start to show his feelings just like a woman, and his strength will decline. For one reason, his validation as a man will come from women, not from men. His measure of manhood will be the female standard, not a male's. His nature will be, as Levant admits, softened.

## Exceptions don't negate the rule.

Feminists who assert that masculinity is primarily nurture and that there is no innate masculinity or femininity cite rare cultures that buck the norm as proof that there are no universals. Among all the cultures that have a masculine ideal of man as the protector, two exceptions seem to reject that notion: Tahiti in French Polynesia and Semai of Malaysia. Paul Gauguin traveled to Tahiti and observed that the people were androgynous with a kind of masculine virility in the women "and something feminine in the men."[67] Researchers who have studied the people of Tahiti have found that, there, the men aren't any more aggressive than the women, and the women weren't any more maternal than the men. They performed the same tasks, and there is no cultural expectation of proving one's manhood. The men have no problem behaving in effeminate ways: "During dances, for instance, adult men will dance together in close bodily contact, rubbing against each other without any anxiety," Gilmore writes, "and most men visit the village homosexual frequently and without shame."[68]

The men of Tahiti had no desire to protect the women. When Westerners came ashore in the past, the women gave themselves freely to the sailors, earning the island the reputation of cheap eroticism. The men of Tahiti sat back and didn't care. They didn't hunt. They didn't do any dangerous occupations. There were no wars, and few worked hard. They were content to live in poverty. The focal point of a village was a single gay transsexual who men and boys visited freely and frequently. When used or taken advantage of by others, the men didn't retaliate. Some Christian missionaries found the passivity of the Tahitians godly—though this is hardly what the Scriptures describe as godly. Quite the opposite, since hard work, defending women and children, and striving for excellence are all biblical values.

The other cultural exception is the Semai people. They were once a more dominant people in the region, but invaders over the years defeated and displaced them, forcing them to live among the hills. The Semai are tiny in stature and choose to run away at any threat rather than fight. They are so passive that researchers have wondered if there's any aggressive impulse in them at all. They believe that even to resist someone who attacks them is to be aggressive. As a result, foreigners find it easy to target Semai women because they will never resist when sexual advances are made, and the men will do nothing to protect the women. Among the Semai, there is no private ownership. They arm themselves and sometimes hunt, which is the extent of their masculine distinctiveness. Interestingly, only men hunt. They use a blowpipe, which they treasure almost as if it is a sign of their manliness.

Do these two examples prove that men don't have to be masculine but can become androgynous along with women? I don't think so. It's significant to note that, in both societies, women don't take on traditionally masculine roles, such as hunting and protecting. The women are still "feminine," but the men are not masculine. They are decidedly effeminate. As Gilmore points out, there are some similarities that "allow" for this state of existence in these two societies. Both have plenty of natural resources, so they don't need to compete for food. They don't face any real threats from the outside world—and, if they do, they're compliant. Instead of nurturing masculinity, they flee like little children.

Feminists and those who reject universal masculinity point to these examples and argue that the mere existence proves that masculinity isn't universal because, if something isn't applicable in all cases, then it can't be called universal. Here we have two instances in which masculinity is not valued in culture. Therefore, masculinity must not be universal, they claim. Sounds reasonable, right? No, it's not. Just because a culture denies masculinity doesn't negate its universal existence. This is because masculinity is present in those cultures—it's just untrained. Masculinity is rooted in a man's psychological and spiritual identity as well as in his purpose. It is a seed in every boy that needs to be watered. It matures through external training, intervention, and initiation rooted in universal values. Without it, men grow, but they remain immature children. It's no surprise that the Tahitians and Semai are described as juvenile in their manner. They are like children, having failed to develop—not only as men and women but as human beings.

Women naturally develop as women—their bodies taking over for them to transition from a girl to a woman. They don't have to work at it. They have to work on their attitudes about it, but not femininity itself. Boys are a different story. Their manhood is active and external. They have to be trained in manliness and initiated into manhood. This doesn't mean they are born sex-neutral. The innate masculine traits are there but underdeveloped. A boy who grows up in a society that has rejected the responsibilities and values of one's male identity will never grow into manhood. Why would he need to? In the same way, a boy can be trained wrongly to develop dysfunctional masculinity that is unhealthy. This often happens when women do the training of boys instead of men initiating them into manhood. The job of making boys into men is given to men because they alone have the masculine nature to develop it in their sons. Women don't. When it comes to masculinity, mature men know best how to make the seeds of masculinity grow. Whether that seed develops into a healthy oak is up to the men in a child's life.

A man's manhood is his identity, given to him by God. For some, that identity is disrupted before he's even born. We live in a broken and fallen world, and babies are born all the time with dysfunctions mentally and physically. For most, that masculine identity is in place, but it must blossom through years of watering and caretaking. Boys are like Bonsai trees that are pruned and shaped into beautiful works of art. Those who receive the nourishment, encouragement, guidance, and initiation necessary to become healthy men will beautifully reflect their masculine identity, so they can care for others, create new things that will benefit humanity, solve life's problems, cultivate the earth, and spread love. A man exists to lead others to be the best they can be and build societies that are secure, good, and reflective of God's abundant love for his creation. Essential to cultivating nature is guarding and protecting it—this includes women.

The Tahitians and Semai lost all sense of protection because they lost a sense of their purpose as human beings and as men. As the image-bearers of God, we're designed to do more than lounge on a beach, have sex with the transsexual in the center of town, and let men rape women. Researchers say these groups became emasculated because threats ceased, and life became easy. Luxury played a role, but there have been plenty of peaceful societies that still exude vitality and masculinity because they haven't been corrupted by laziness and selfishness. This is the challenge of "soft" technologically advanced societies. Our goal shouldn't be to reconstruct masculinity into a feminized version because life is a breeze but to press forward with strength and vitality out of love and service to others. The ease of the Tahitians and Semai didn't cause their emasculation, but it did perpetuate it. All societies that find themselves in times of ease need to be aware of the temptation to stop living according to one's purpose. Essential to being human is moral and mental development. Men are rational creatures made to use their minds, not simply exist. They are artists fashioned to create, inventors equipped to discover, warriors trained to protect, and creatures blessed with free will to go on life's great adventure.

If you are moving, working, discovering, and creating in this life—if you are living as you are called to live—then you will face resistance. Hardship will come from nature, if nothing else. Even if you live in the most technologically advanced society full of ease and comfort—the "soft" society Levant says is ushering in softer masculinity—there is a battle that never ends. It is the battle between good and evil. This is a battle the Tahitians and Semai succumbed to. As human beings, our highest goal is to love others, and sin has no place in love. The highest calling of a man is to love a woman, if not in marriage then as a male serving his purpose in society for the benefit of women. The highest calling of any individual is to love the God who made him unique, gifted with special abilities and talents to contribute to society like no one else.

To be the people we are called to be is a moral calling. We cannot do it if we are awash in harmful behavior, engaging in soul-damaging activities, living only for ourselves as if we are our own gods, and fixated on material ease or gain. The battle we wage is ever-present. Bad people exist. We have our own badness to conquer. This battle translates into very real challenges that can only be truly overcome when both men and women are living according to their purpose. Men as warriors, with insight and male intuition, can lead that battle by discerning threats derived from our own choices or deployed by others and defeating them. When children are tempted to stray, fathers have powerful influence to deter them through discipline and correction. Mothers can do this too, but good, strong fathers have a presence in the face of conflict and defiance that stops a child in his tracks. Just ask any mom who has been with her children all day. Dad comes home and everyone shapes up—immediately.

Men have an unemotional approach to dealing with conflict that puts them above the fray instead of becoming entangled in it. This is a powerful ability that is necessary when dealing with other people. We might be at ease because of our technology, but people are still turbulent and destructive. Just look at our politics—our culture is drowning in strife. We need strong men to grab our society by its arms, coolly get it under control, and make it see reason again.

## SOMETIMES PROTECTING WOMEN IS PROTECTING THEM FROM THEMSELVES AND TAKING THE HITS.

Because of childhood abuse and further trauma as an adult, I suffer from complex post-traumatic stress disorder (CPTSD). Like people with PTSD, I get triggered when I feel threatened, though I don't relive the details of my trauma like those with PTSD. I get lost in fight-or-flight modes, abandoning all rational thought to instinct and fear. When I have an episode, everything goes red. Life alternately rushes by and moves in slow motion in a filter of scarlet haze. My heart races and fear courses through every fiber of my being.

One time, my husband and I were visiting Asheville, North Carolina. I lived there long ago, and it was the setting of another traumatic event in my life. I probably shouldn't have returned, but we thought I'd be fine. I wasn't. While we were dining at a restaurant, we got into an argument and my CPTSD erupted. Flight took over, and I ran from the restaurant. I didn't know where I was going. I just ran down the main street, along a back alley somewhere, through bushes and buildings. Lights, scents, noises filled the darkness around me, an onslaught of stimuli that was eventually lost in the red haze. I found myself outside of a hotel. It wasn't my hotel, but I decided to go in and find a room. I couldn't tell you why. As I was waiting at the counter, my heart still banging in my chest, I saw my husband outside. I went out to confront him, though I don't know what about. My flight turned to fight.

Somehow, he steered me into the shadows of the hotel and tried to calm me, but I wouldn't settle down. I was yelling, ripping plants from planters and throwing them at him. I screamed at the imaginary ghosts that haunted me. I ran at him and started scratching and punching. He calmly took it, finally reaching out and taking my arms, folding them across my chest and pulling me toward him. The red haze didn't lift, and I continued to cry in rage. He held me close, patiently, lovingly, with self-controlled strength.

Somewhere amid the haze, I felt his arms around me. I saw his face as if he had stepped out of a storm, and I could see him clearly, my tears like rain on my cheeks. I could feel the night air cooling them. I could feel my husband's body, strong as I slumped into him. He held me until I was calm, stroking my hair, drying my tears. When I fully came out of it, I was ashamed. Such breaks rarely happen, but, when they do, all I feel is shame. He didn't deserve to be treated that way. I even entertained the thought that he should have hit me back just because I deserved it. But that would never happen. He showed manly strength and restraint when I lost myself. As my emotions unleashed, he roped his in. As I became caged with fear, he set me free with love.

It's not easy to share this story with you. It's embarrassing. I'm sure I'll be mocked for my mental illness—I've experienced that on occasion. As much as we think we're past stigmatizing mental illness, we're not. But I need to show you an example of a man being a man in one of the most intimate moments. It's no surprise that my husband's favorite movie is *To Kill a Mockingbird.* He admires the strength, goodness, and restraint of Atticus Finch. My husband very much reflects those qualities. If a dog comes into town and threatens his family, he'll shoot it dead. If his daughter is troubled, he'll pull her into his lap and comfort her. If he needs to stand against a mob for the sake of righteousness, he'll do it, no matter the harm that comes to him. He'll take the hits of injustice and face the onslaught because it is the right thing to do, and it is his job, his purpose, to do just that. If he were taught to express his emotions at every turn, he couldn't have been the rock I need to cling to during the storm.

One of the most profound aches of a man's soul in these "softer times" is the loss of his value as defender and protector. Men still fight and defend, but it's not appreciated the way it once was. If anything, a man's strength is looked upon with suspicion. He's told he needs to be more emotional and less aggressive. More cooperative and less competitive. More of a girly man than a manly man. Any man who struggles with these expectations isn't "toxic." He's a normal, healthy man who wants to be himself and respected for it. Yes, these are softer times because of technology. Yes, men have to do more chores around the house because Mom is at work. But life is still full of danger. Threats are always around the corner. Women still need their knights to defend them. Evil must still be conquered. Women still need men to be men.

CHAPTER 7

# MEN AS LOVERS (WOMEN'S BOOBS ARE AWESOME)

*There is the heat of Love, the pulsing rush of Longing, the lover's whisper, irresistible— magic to make the sanest man go mad.*

—Homer

It had been a long, busy day. I was tired with six kids running around, tugging, pulling, and yelling. Summers weren't vacations for me, and I wanted school to begin again so I'd have peace and time alone for myself. I was also stressed with work, editing for a medical research contractor. The deadlines were closing in, and I hadn't finished half of my assignment. The house was a wreck, but I wanted it clean before my husband came home—not because he demanded it, but because I wanted to make home peaceful for him, a haven after he worked all day. Walking in the front door to stumble over toys and mounds of laundry isn't exactly relaxing. So

I cleaned, occupied the kids with some toys and coloring projects, finished off an assignment, and made dinner.

Around six, my husband came home. I had dinner ready, fed everyone, cleaned up the kitchen, and went upstairs to shower. As the warm water flowed over me, I realized I hadn't spoken to another adult all day. No conversation, no feelings shared, no adult stimulation. I had been on the go since dawn—in silence, except for talking with my children. I was looking forward to spending time with my husband, getting the adult refueling I needed, venting my thoughts about the day. That didn't happen. Wrapped in my bathrobe, I walked into the bedroom and found him asleep. He had a long day of business meetings, negotiating deals, making decisions about how to spend marketing monies. He's not much of an extrovert by nature, so his job drained him. I watched as he breathed deeply, his face relaxed. I kissed him gently on the forehead. Dimming the light, I slipped into my nightgown and climbed into bed with a book I knew wouldn't be open for long. As I turned the first page, I felt my husband stir. He touched my arm and pulled me to him. I rolled over to see his sleepy eyes warm with longing. I knew what he wanted. He didn't even have to speak.

I don't know why—maybe it was the example my mother set for me in her relationship with my dad, maybe it's my intuition, maybe it's because I was confident in his love for me, but I knew—as I always did—that his desire for sex wasn't just a physical drive born of selfish lust. He wasn't thoughtless and greedy. He needed to connect. He needed the comfort of my body. I didn't feel like it, but I wanted to be the one to meet his needs, to touch him in a way no one else could, and to satisfy him. So I crawled on top of him and kissed him passionately, letting him know I was present and willing. Our eyes connected, our bodies joined, and we communicated love without words. Afterward, as I fell asleep in his arms, he whispered, "I love you, treasure." At that moment, that's all I needed.

Not every day was like that, of course. We have reciprocity in our marriage. My husband talks to me when he comes home, even though he's worn out from the day and the last thing he wants to do is utter another word, listen to another rant, or make another decision. He does it because he loves me, just as I make love to him even when I'm tired and don't feel like it. I wish more marriages could experience this intimacy without words. It's a joy like nothing else.

Men have a lot to say on this topic, as you can imagine. They range from how to deal with sex in marriage to how to interact with girls these days without contracts and consent forms.

"Stop expecting us to read your minds about what you want. Tell us what you want in the bedroom. Tell us what you need. We'll do it!—and listen to us when we tell you what we need. Sometimes that's doing something new, if you're comfortable with it."

"Women are so aggressive. How about you let me be in the driver's seat for a while? And when I do take it, don't falsely accuse me of abusing you."

"Don't expect us to act like women in the bedroom."

"Be feminine, please. Be sexy. Is that so hard?"

"Women do lie about rape sometimes. It's true. Deal with it."

"A healthy sex life doesn't mean you have to be a whore."

"You're beautiful. But if you show off your skin and curves, guys are going to look. That doesn't make them pervs; it's how they're wired."

"I'd love to be able to say to a random girl that I see as I walk by, 'Wow, you have beautiful eyes,' not to hit on her, but just as a compliment. Whatever happened to gentlemen complimenting ladies in public? Oh that's right—SJWs say it's rape."

"If you're wearing yoga pants, don't get offended if I check out your booty."

"Stop having sex with losers. If you won't have his baby, don't have sex with him."

"Ladies. The vast majority of us do not see you as 'sex objects.' What we hope from you is kindness, understanding, and acceptance."

"Wanting to have sex with my wife after a long day's work is not being insensitive. It's how I reconnect with her."

"Women, get off the 'all men are rapists and abusers' train. Quit acting like flirting is harassment. It waters down real harassment."

## IF YOU LOVE YOUR MAN, GIVE HIM WHAT HE NEEDS.

One time, as I'm prone to do, I discussed the topic of sex on social media, and I tweeted that women need to make love to their husbands even when they don't feel like it. The backlash from feminists was swift and vicious. "How dare you make a woman a sex slave!!!" "You're setting women back!" "We're not here to serve men!" The feminists were wailing as if I had chained them to bedposts. You'd have thought these women were in abusive relationships, but they weren't, and I wasn't talking about marriages that are riddled with strife, neglect, and cruelty. I was talking about relatively healthy marriages in which two people love each other—and that was my assumption—love.

The sad thing is how many women fail to be a resting place for their husbands. Too often, a wife demands that her husband express his feelings daily like a woman, but she is physically absent when he needs to express himself. A man's heart and body are very much tied together when it comes to his feelings. The greatest emotional release and expression for him is sex. He shows his wife love and his need for her with his body as well as his words. Women need to understand that when a man says, "Can we have sex tonight?" he's looking for connection. It might not be through words, but it's with his body joining with hers.

I know it's popular to instruct men on all the ways to woo a woman throughout the day to get her into bed at night. Flowers, love notes, long conversations, and even a good house cleaning. This is all well and good, but how about women take some steps to love a man as he needs to be loved? Sometimes that means having sex with him when he needs it, even if he hasn't jumped through hoops all day. If you're in a loving relationship, then you don't need to be convinced your husband loves you to "reward" him with sex.

Sex is love, and love is sex in the marriage bond. To use it as a bargaining tool or, worse, a weapon to punish him through neglect is selfish and destroys love. In some Jewish circles, neglect of sex is cause for divorce because the "oneness" of the covenant, which is both spiritual and physical, has been broken. I know Christians who could learn a thing or two from their Jewish brothers and sisters on this point. If you love the man you're married to, *make love* to him. See him as he is, not as you expect him to be. A woman can love a man best by being present physically, so the gateway to his heart is opened through sex, instead of demanding that he come to her as an emotional reflection of herself.

## WITH SEXUAL FREEDOM COMES PERSONAL RESPONSIBILITY.

Neglect of sex in marriage isn't the only problem men are dealing with these days. The tables have flipped in the dating world, with women often the hunter and men the prey. They're like the actress Natalie Dormer in the video "Someone New" by Hozier, where she prowls through the night looking for one sexual encounter after another. She's always searching, but the joining is only physical. She isn't satisfied because she doesn't ever connect, and so she goes on searching for someone new. Men (being men) don't complain about this much, but it has disrupted relational dynamics, as women have become the aggressors. This role reversal has created an environment of mixed signals, lack of trust, false accusation, and irresponsibility. I hate to sound like a prude, but there are consequences for free sex. The problem is, many women don't want to deal with them. They don't want to take responsibility for their sexual freedom. My goal isn't to rob women of sexual liberty, but to hold them to account for it, to remind them that they are human beings who need to be responsible for their choices.

I say this not as one who has lived a prim and proper life. I say it as a woman who has had her share of sexual exploits. One of the worst was committing adultery and getting pregnant as a result. I had to face my choice to have sex and not blame anyone else. Not my husband or the man I fell in love with, and not my church where I had served for years. I had only myself to blame, and, as I pulled into the parking lot of an abortion clinic twenty years ago, I had to face myself and my own abuse of "sexual liberty" and decide whether I was going to grow up and take responsibility for my choices or put the burden on someone else.

I sat in the hot car that day smelling old French fries. There were always some under the seat where the kids spilled them, but the kids were gone now. I didn't know where. I looked through the grimy windshield at the abortion clinic in front of me. It beckoned me, like a ghost. Sweat was running down the back of my neck, but I didn't turn on the air conditioner. I wanted to feel the heat. I wanted the distraction from the pain. My hand strayed to my stomach. I was more than two months pregnant. Still time to kill the baby. And killing was what it was. No one could tell me otherwise. I'd had two children. I'd lost two others. I knew what it was like to feel a child grow inside of me. The little twitches of life, the turning of an elbow or a knee as it rolled across my stomach, or the flutter of faint hiccups.

I watched as a young girl and her friend hurried from their car to the building. They slipped inside, with the door banging behind them; I wondered which of them was pregnant. I looked in the mirror. I was thirty-three. Hardly a teenager. I didn't recognize the woman in the mirror. I saw only shame. I wanted to get out of the car, but I couldn't stop thinking about that hospital in Florida six years before. I'd been rushed to the emergency room. I was bleeding, and they were rolling me into the ultrasound room to be examined. The room was freezing and I couldn't stop shaking. The technician spread jelly across my stomach and turned on the machine. I expected to see my baby dead, his heartbeat silent, his body still. I'd seen that before, and I braced for it. But God had other plans.

My son was alive and well, his little feet moving. His heartbeat was steady. I stared at him, thankful to be able to peer into his world, to see him safe and sound inside of me. I never felt love like I felt at that moment. A mother's love. So pure. So natural. His features were undeveloped. His fingers fragile, his toes so tiny. But he was my son, and I knew he would grow up to bring happiness to others. The ache I felt at that moment was one of expectation, longing, and inexpressible joy. Very different from the ache I felt as

I sat in the hot car outside of the abortion clinic. I felt no joy, no longing, no hope. Only despair and a desperate desire to fix what I'd broken and to get my life back.

I'd separated from my husband. A selfish choice. Oh, I could tell you a thousand reasons—many of them understandable, maybe even justified, but it doesn't matter. The bottom line was I'd separated and had begun a new life, one with another man. It wasn't long before I knew I couldn't live with that choice. My two children meant too much to me. Children are supposed to live in a stable home where they grow in the confidence and assurance of both their parents' love. I couldn't live with the sadness I saw in them since the separation, during those weeks they stayed with me before returning to visit their father. Their confusion and their fear were burdens I didn't want them to bear any longer. So I decided to reconcile.

There was also my church. I had left it too—another broken part of my life I needed to fix. I had been publicly excommunicated, shunned. Church members weren't allowed to eat with me. When I saw them in town, they turned the other way. They saw me as an untouchable, no longer a Christian, no longer a mother. Unforgiven. Cast out. I deserved it. I believed that. I accepted my punishment, but then the church went too far. They wanted to take away my children, sever my relationship with them as if I'd never existed. I'd received several letters from leaders in the church that my divorce meant I was no longer a mother to my children. If I broke the covenant of marriage, I wasn't allowed to enjoy the privileges of the covenant—being a mother. In other words, if I left my husband, I had to leave my children as well. I was no longer a mother in the eyes of the church or of God. I didn't believe that, but I felt powerless. I wanted my children in my life, just as I wanted them to be with their father, but the church wouldn't tolerate a divorce. It was all or nothing.

I had received a letter just that week from an elder's wife, telling me that if I chose to divorce then I needed to do the "honorable thing" and stay completely separate from my children until by God's grace I repent and live by faith in obedience to God. My husband had also written to me after he had picked up the children that I was to "sever all communication and contact with them: no more visits, no phone calls, no emails, and no letters." He said I was no longer the mother of these children. I read those letters many times, and I knew what I had to do—not just because of the threats, but because I loved my children. I wanted them happy again. At peace.

I'll never forget the day I returned. I went to the elders and begged for forgiveness. I wanted to tell them the reasons I'd left, such as neglect in my marriage—surely, some of them would understand—but I didn't. I kept quiet. I knew what I had to do, and I was willing to do it. I was willing to make everything right again. We sat in a dimly lit classroom at the church. Six men and me. A tribunal of sorts. Bibles open before us. The anger in the room was palpable. So was the grief. The fluorescent lights overhead blinked, and it was raining outside. Streams poured down the windows in thick curvy lines, and thunder echoed through the mountains. The men listened to me and said they would give me the help I needed to fix my marriage, to make my family whole again—if I complied with their admonitions and requirements. I would be a mother again under the authority of my husband and the church.

I went back to my apartment to gather my things but, there was a problem—I was pregnant. I had worried about it for days and put off the test, but I couldn't live in denial forever. I sat in the bathroom on the floor, my knees pulled up to my chin, and I watched as the red line turned into a cross, confirming what I already knew. My world shattered. I was at a crossroads. I couldn't keep my baby and fix my marriage. I couldn't keep my baby and have my children returned to me. Even then, I didn't know where they were. They were either with the church people or out of town. I didn't know. My husband hadn't told me. He had simply taken them and said I was no longer their mother, that I was dead to them. I wondered if he had told them I'd died. Part of me wished he had.

I wrestled with what to do, but I knew some things couldn't be fixed. Sometimes we shatter things so badly that all the pieces can't be put together again, no matter how we try. I was going to lose a child somehow. No matter what choice I made, there would be loss—and not just my loss, my children's loss. They would lose a mother. Everything had changed for them. Nothing would be right or whole. I had created a difficult situation through my own choices that brought pain—to everyone. The shame, the isolation, and the guilt were overwhelming.

I considered giving the baby up for adoption, but the father wouldn't hear of it. He would raise the child. But the church and my husband refused to accept that. I would not be allowed back to raise my two children, to restore my family, as long as I knew where my illegitimate baby was. The only choice was to deliver the baby, and someone (a person from the church or my husband—I didn't know the details of the plan) would take her from me without me ever seeing her. I would sign over legal rights and they would give her up for adoption. I could do that because, according to the law, the father had no legal right to the child since we weren't married.

But I couldn't do it. I knew the father would fight it—a battle I didn't want to face. I didn't even know if I could give my baby up for adoption. How could I live with her alive in this world, alone? My child? One day, she would grow up and she would wonder why I rejected her. I couldn't bear to think of it. Maybe if I'd never raised children of my own, I could do it. But I was a mother. I knew what it was like to hold my child at my breast, smell her new baby smells, feel the softness of her skin. I knew what it was like to hear her first words and see the wonder in her eyes when she swam for the first time, or ate her first ice cream, or learned to read her first word.

The tangled web of emotions and consequences was a noose I couldn't escape. That's when I thought about abortion. Killing the baby. It would fix everything. How ironic—how twisted—that I couldn't bear the thought of adoption, but I could contemplate death. Yet, in that moment of darkness, I thought it was the best choice. It would be so easy. Millions of women did it every year—death for a convenient life—the legacy of sex-positive feminism. My life could go on like it had before. My marriage would be whole. My children would have their mother again. God would forgive me. The church would accept me back. My family would be together. My children would be happy. But my baby would be dead. Could I sacrifice this child on the altar of my selfishness? This beautiful child growing inside of me? A child I was responsible for? A baby I had brought into existence by my own choice to have sex?

The car was like a furnace, and I looked at the door to the abortion clinic through the haze of heat on the hood. The smell of stale fries brought back memories of my children laughing, of days when everything was good. Maybe not perfect. But good. It could be that way again. Just step out of the car, keep the appointment, lie down on the table, close my eyes, spread my legs, and let them cut out my mistake.

I opened the car door and walked across the parking lot to the entrance. The sky was so blue and birds were singing, but all I heard was my heart beating. All I could see was the blurry haze of the building in front of me. I stepped inside as a bell on the door jingled, and I felt a wave of cold air wash over me. A woman sitting behind the desk looked up. "Can I help you?" she asked. I glanced around the room. The girls who had entered earlier were sitting off to the side. One was flipping through a magazine. The other looked up at me. Her eyes were filled with tears. We looked at each other—a shared moment of guilt, of compassion, of pain—and then she turned away. I couldn't move.

"Miss, can I help you?" the woman at the desk repeated.

I shook my head. "No. I'm sorry. No, you can't." I left and ran to the car. I can still hear the bell on the door ringing. I started the engine and pulled out of the parking lot. I couldn't do it. I couldn't kill my child on account of my own miserable mistakes. I didn't know what I was going to do—I didn't know what I had the strength to do—but I had to accept the consequences of my choices. I couldn't end a life to make my life easier or better. I had to face my pain. Grief is the result of wrong choices. Suffering is the consequence of sin. If we're willing to sin, we need to be willing to accept the suffering that comes with it. To run from it, to do even worse things to avoid it—piling one wrong upon another—is no answer. It only causes more pain, more suffering—maybe not for you, but certainly for the child you've killed.

I didn't kill my daughter. I'm ashamed that I wanted to—even for a moment. In the end, though, I couldn't do it. Her blood would not be spilled to make my life easier, no matter how right my motivations might have been when it came to my family. Choosing life changed my world forever. It was never the same, and it has been difficult as I've struggled to navigate the waters of a broken life. Women who abort their children do it because they say they want a better life. But it's not a better life they want—it's an easier one. It's a life without outward struggle, without the consequences of choices already made. It is easier. But it's not better. Death is never better.

If I had chosen to abort my baby, I would have chosen death. Blood spilled to wash away my sins. Another's life taken so I could have mine, so I could be free of the consequences of my choice to have sex. But the blood of a child can never fix what is broken. That sacrifice is a lie. The only blood that can bring life has already been spilled. That red line has already been crossed, and it wasn't in a dark bathroom as I lay curled on a floor. It wasn't on a surgical table at an abortion clinic. It was on a hill far away and long ago. A sacrifice already made. A life already given so we can live ours—not free of pain—but free of guilt and full of joy.[69]

Instead of death, I chose a new life, albeit a broken one. I sought a divorce—justified on account of my adultery—and appealed to my husband for shared custody, finalizing details of child support in the courts. In a different time and a different age before first-wave feminism, I might not have had that legal freedom. Adultery used to be a crime under which women suffered more than men, and the state might have denied me rights to my children just the church had decreed. But early feminists fought for political and individual liberty and challenged such laws that deprived women of the same liberties as a man. I applaud that legacy, despite the difficulties freedom creates when we use it for selfish ends. Individual freedom does not free us from personal responsibilities, and in a situation that could not be fixed without a child being totally deprived of her parents, I sought what was best in an imperfect situation. I wanted all my children to have access to their parents, to grow up knowing they were loved by both, and to be free to love them back.

Focusing on the path ahead, I gathered up my two children and moved to Charlotte, unable to be in a town of shunning, an environment of constant oppression for my children and me. Never breaking his visitation even while living in separate cities, my soon-to-be ex-husband followed later where we mutually cared for our children under a joint custody arrangement. I married the father of my baby, raising her with her brothers and sisters and the love of her parents. I wish the situation could have been whole. I wish it could have been easy for everyone, but it wasn't. It was a difficult path, but it's one I had to own, take responsibility for as best I could, and not blame others for my sin, just as I couldn't deny my children a relationship with their mother or my daughter her life because of my sexual choices.

## SEXUAL LIBERTY HAS REDUCED WOMEN TO OBJECTS FOR SEX—THE VERY THING WOMEN SOUGHT TO ESCAPE.

Nothing gets feminists more riled up than sharing stories like this and telling women to take personal responsibility for their actions. Even talking about sex in a way that holds a woman accountable sends many of them into a hissy fit. While it was good to free women from legal barriers to their sexual expression, it has never been good to free women from moral accountability of those same sexual expressions. Feminists today want to be released from any sort of principled compass that imposes moral judgments on their sexual liberty. Instead of taking responsibility for their own freedoms, it's just always easier to blame the man and treat him as the predator, even though outside of rape, women are active participants in making those moral (or not so moral) choices.

I once tweeted that "My greatest regret is giving my body over to unworthy men because it made me feel good about myself to get a sexual response from a man—a fleeting response that had nothing to do with my value, only my physical ability to stimulate. It meant nothing and cheapened me—and him." I was shocked by the reaction to this moment of honesty and vulnerability. Many people said it was brave of me to admit that a life of sexual "liberty" wasn't all it was cracked up to be. I didn't think it was very brave to confess my failures, just honest. Others accused me of being disturbed—sex, in any context, is awesome, they said. How wrong they were. Along with these naysayers were many men and women who echoed my feelings. The promises of the sexual revolution have led to pain, disconnection, and regret as an intimate act designed to create life and intimacy within the marital bond has been reduced to an animalistic urge to be indulged with every craving. Sex has become about power and self-indulgence, not committed love—and love is what sets us apart from mere animals.

With the women's liberation movement, feminists celebrated freedom from previous conventionalities and the perimeters set by a "patriarchal" society, moving women's "rights" far beyond the quest for individual liberty before the law and the attainment of liberties enjoyed by men to a break from moral absolutes and responsibilities. The sexual liberation of later feminists was rooted in the desire to be free to express themselves any way they wished with no social consequences to those choices. They sought to take control of their own sexual destinies and identities. No longer would women allow men to objectify them and define their sexuality. Women would express their sexuality as they wanted, even if that meant sleeping with one man after another like a character out of *Girls* or *Sex and the City*. Sadly, in their quest to be free from the objectification of men, women now objectify themselves. And by doing so, guess what? Men still objectify women. If a woman is constantly posting her bare breasts on social media in the name of empowerment, she can't cry foul when men respond to her as a sexual object. She has put that aspect of her private self on full display, identifying herself first and foremost by her intense sexuality. She'll claim she isn't. Or she says that at least she's doing it on her terms, so she can reveal the breadth of her identity as she determines. "There's more to me than my naked body," she says. Yes, there is, but that's not what's presented. What men see first is her naked body—and, for a man, that is a powerful thing.

Women know the power of their bodies, which is why they flaunt them. They like the sexual control they wield over men, but women want to do it on their terms—not a man's. That's understandable to a degree, but women need to realize that, even when they use their sexuality "on their own terms," they can't control how a man responds. His reactions are "on his terms," and a woman isn't going to change that—and I'm not talking about rape, which is never acceptable. When a woman objectifies herself, her narrative about autonomy gets away from her. When she exposes her bare body for whatever personal reason she claims, a normal, healthy man will look at her sexually. He will even be tempted to lust after her. In other words, the woman is objectified. Whether it's by her choice or another's, it doesn't matter. She has been reduced to her material form despite there being so much more to her.

I stepped into another social media quagmire when I brought up this point, calling women to account for their sexual choices and telling them that, if they're going to get all dolled up with glossy lips and lubed legs, they can't blame men for the consequences—particularly pregnancy. The reaction was a deluge of criticism and hate. Five media outlets from the United Kingdom, including the *Daily Mail*, asked me what could I possibly mean by saying such a terrible thing. I made it clear to them. I support a woman having a right to have sex as much and as freely as she wants. I'm not saying everyone who puts on makeup is on the prowl for sex. I am saying that women get dressed up, don seduction like armor, and go on the "hunt" to have sex, and if they're going to do that, they need to be responsible for what happens and not put the blame on men. Again, I'm not talking about rape or sexual assault. I'm talking about the consequences of cooperative sex—diseases, broken relationships, heartache, and pregnancy. As for the lubed legs—which seemed to drive people crazy—I just meant oiled. My critics were thinking KY Jelly; I was thinking coconut oil. Shiny things attract attention, and women like to attract attention when they're looking for sex. Women want men, and men want women. It's a tale as old as time; the only difference now is that women want their freedom without responsibility.

## WE ARE TRAPPED IN A MYTH OF SEXUAL EQUALITY.

Despite "acting" like men when it comes to sexual conquests, women are still who they are. They can't shed their designed identity. They didn't create themselves, so they can't recreate themselves into something else. Their feminine nature is still very much a part of them, whether they like it or not. The purpose of a woman's sexuality hasn't changed, even though she uses, misuses, and abuses it in the name of freedom. Her body is still made to receive a man. Her body is still made to get pregnant—a concern for fertile women no matter the method of birth control. Her body is still weaker than a man's. She remains as vulnerable as she ever has been. Her need to be emotionally connected through sex is still a part of her psyche, unless she has completely severed her heart from the act of sex—something that is particularly damaging to women because of their vulnerability as the receiver in sex.

The myth of sexual equality has driven a dagger through healthy sex. The more women think they're the same as men, the more they realize they aren't. This creates fear in the heart of the woman. She has set herself up as if she can approach sex just like a man only to become keenly aware that he is more powerful and that the consequences are more internal for a woman (babies are made). Instead of stepping back and accepting the sexual differences between men and women, she determines that he's naturally sexually threatening, even prone to abuse. She treats him like a wild animal that must be tamed and caged, heaping guilt onto him for all his natural masculine attractions and feelings.

A man now can't even admire a woman's sexiness without being made to feel like he's "ogling" her and raping her with his eyes. Natural sexual tensions are deemed abusive, and men are expected not to see women as sexual creatures, even as ladies post pics of themselves as sexual objects to be seen by men, even as they wear sexy clothing to work, and even as they doll themselves up with full lips, long eyelashes, and flushed cheeks. There's nothing inherently wrong with this, and feminine beauty is sexual beauty, but we can't change the reality that this image stirs a man at his most primal level. He is morally obligated to control his response, but we are deluded if we expect sexually healthy men to emote like eunuchs.

Mixed messages by women—along with false threats of sexual harassment or abuse when a man responds to a woman's sexual display—have men scratching their heads and wondering what they should actually be doing with women. Can't a man merely admire a woman's sexual beauty, even be attracted to it, comment on it, and point out to his friends how desirous a woman is without being made to feel like a criminal? As one man told me, "We aren't all perverted rapists waiting for you to let your guard down. Sometimes we just admire you—and, yeah, there's some desire in that, but that doesn't make us monsters."

Women need to give men a break and not take their attraction to beautiful women as a threat. If a man looks at you and recognizes your sexual beauty and even says something a little naughty (depending on the context), leave him alone. He's not threatening you. He's a man—he might need a dose of self-control in how to express himself, but he's not hurting you. He's complimenting you. Likewise, if you're with a man and he notices another beautiful woman, don't get defensive—unless he lingers, of course. He's being a healthy male.

I recently bought a poster Farrah Fawcett for my husband's man cave because—like millions of other guys in the seventies—he had the poster in his bedroom as a teenager. The red bathing suit, the hair, and that smile are iconic. It's now a point of nostalgia. I wanted him to have it for that reason, and a beautiful picture of a woman in my husband's man cave doesn't threaten me. He didn't know her personally. It's more like a work of art. It's beautiful. I should let him enjoy that, especially since it's tied to a memory of days gone by—even if it stirs his loins in a passing moment (men, after all, are men). Of course, if he had pictures of women he's in contact with or cam girls looking to titillate, if he had porn on his laptop, or if he had a lust problem, that would be another issue. But my husband exercises self-control, he loves me, and this is a healthy situation—one that I can feel comfortable with because I celebrate my husband's masculinity and his appreciation of feminine beauty. I appreciate it too!

Too many men aren't free to be their usual sexual selves. They're either expected to man-whore around with women in the name of sexual liberty or told to stop looking at women and treat them like nuns. It's all very confusing. Men have a lot of pent-up frustrations when it comes to sex in our feminized American culture—ironic when we're expected to be enjoying the "sexual liberty" promised by the sexual revolution. But this so-called liberty has become a cage because we've separated sex from its designed purpose of wholeness within a trusted relationship bound by a promise.

## A FEW BAD MEN DON'T MAKE ALL MEN BAD.

When I said earlier in the book that I've seen men at their worst and their best, this is true in the area of sex more than any other. When I was young, I was molested by a boy several years older than me. At the age of sixteen, I was sexually harassed by a customer while working at a local drug store. I was raped in college and sexually harassed by a client when I worked in advertising. I've been inappropriately hit on more times than I can count in my work as a political commentator. I won't go so far as to call it harassment, but some women might. I've talked to many women about their own #MeToo moments in which men have stepped over lines or been outright abusive. I know the damage men who have not matured as the loving masculine males they're designed to be can cause.

Right now, however, I don't want to dwell on the immaturity of men in this area. I address men's failures and struggles in Chapter 8. Instead, I want to talk about most men—sexually healthy men who are frustrated for all the right reasons, starting with the issue of rape and sexual abuse. A lie has been circulating in popular culture and academics for some time now that there is a rape culture on college campuses. This has been debunked, as reliable studies have shown that rape and sexual assault are a lot lower than what's reported in the media. Still, the notion that men are predators waiting to pounce has gained steam among women, so much so that the government has created new regulations to address the issue. Colleges have taken on a greater policing role to clamp down on sex crimes, going so far as to eliminate due process for men who are accused of sexual assault, often with no corroborating evidence.

I spoke to a father who went through the heartbreaking nightmare of trying to prove his son's innocence when falsely accused of rape. Trying to prove a negative—that he did not do something—is impossible. There's a reason our justice system is based on the principle of innocent until proven guilty—and that guilt should involve more than just the victim's testimony. We know women sometimes lie about rape—and, yes, they do. As tragic as it is, rape victims should be treated the same as any other victim. We don't (or at least shouldn't) put someone in prison for murder based on one person's uncorroborated testimony. There must be supporting evidence.

That men are targeted not only by women but by a system that has reduced their most basic rights is a travesty that cuts deep into relationships within our society. Trust is necessary to live civilly and freely with one another. By this, I don't mean naive trust. We need discernment to avoid exploitation. I'm talking about generalized trust that isn't eradicated because someone is a member of an identity group. The presumptions that men are predators and that a woman should be believed before a man are devastating to our social cohesion.

The only way women can begin to repair this damage is to take responsibility for their freedom, to understand who men are and how to interpret what they are doing, and to reject both naiveté on the one hand and jaded condemnation on the other. When it comes to our sexual interaction with one another, we need to develop some wisdom. To do that, women must understand who a man is sexually and treat him accordingly—not out of fear, but out of love and respect.

## MEN ARE DEEPLY SENSUAL.

When we hear about a man's sexuality, the first thought we often have is that he's sexually assertive or he's sexually visual. While both of these are true, to one degree or another, a man is primarily *sensual.* No matter his personality, if he is a healthy masculine male, he delights in sensuality in some way. This is part of his nature in all areas of his life. He wants to climb mountains, feel the beat of music, smell the salt of the ocean, touch the smooth frame of a finely built car, and feel his heart pound as he bikes along a sparkling river or competes with other men in sports. He wants to feel alive. The need to physically connect with nature is at the core of a man's being.

When it comes to sex, men are just as sensual. A man wants to engage all of his senses: seeing, hearing, touching, tasting, and smelling. He wants to take in the full beauty of a woman's body, not because he's emotionally disconnected, but because he is deeply sensual. He wants to touch her skin, feel his body press against hers. He wants to taste her salty sweetness as they make love. He wants to smell her hair and skin. He wants to hear her catch her breath at his touch and moan in release. A man is enraptured by feminine beauty. It beckons him to draw closer simply by its very being.

A woman's physical form is a powerful thing. It's a fire that draws a man out of the cold shadows of the world. This attraction doesn't necessarily reduce a woman to a sexual object (though that can happen). For a healthy man, a woman's body is a gateway to her soul, a door he wants to open so he can step through and know every detail about her. That's his natural response, and he feels it stir within when he sees a sexually attractive woman. This doesn't mean he's going to act on it. Married men feel this instinctive attraction too. It's part of them. It's not a license to lust or abuse, but it is present because of his sensual nature. To make a man eradicate this or treat it as inherently evil is to rob him of his sexuality as God designed it. Again, lusting isn't the same thing as appreciating or instinctively responding to a woman. Self-control is the key. Self-denial of one's nature is not. The next time a man notices your sexuality and feminine beauty, don't think he's a creep. Know that he's the sensual creature God made him.

Sensuality is a man's passion. It is the essence of the masculine lover. "The man under the influence of the Lover [psyche] wants to touch and be touched," Moore and Gillette write. "He wants to touch everything physically and emotionally, and he wants to be touched by everything.... He wants to live out the connectedness he feels with the world inside, in the context of his powerful feelings, and outside, in the context of his relationships with other people. Ultimately, he wants to experience the world of sensual experience in its totality."[70]

Most men are true romantics. They are writers of poetry and songs, sweeping epics, and glorious prose that take us on journeys into the hearts and minds of men. Byron, Yeats, Shakespeare, Keats—all lovers who spilled their passion onto the page. "His heart danced upon her movements like a cork upon a tide. He heard what her eyes said to him from beneath her cowl and knew that in some dim past, whether in life or revery, he had heard their tale before," James Joyce writes in *A Portrait of the Artist as a Young Man*.

> With a sudden movement she bowed his head and joined her lips to his and he read the meaning of her movements in her frank uplifted eyes. It was too much for him. He closed his eyes, surrendering himself to her, body and mind, conscious of nothing in the world but the dark pressure of her softly parting lips. They pressed upon his brain as they touched upon his lips as though they were a vehicle of a vague speech; and between them he felt an unknown and timid pressure, darker than the swoon of sin, softer than sound or odor.[71]

I don't know about you, but just reading this makes me swoon.

The masculine lover is an artist who wants to feel everything in a burst of artistic empathy. As Joyce writes in *Ulysses*, "Touch me. Soft eyes. Soft soft soft hand. I am lonely here. O, touch me soon, now. What is that word known to all men? I am quiet here alone. Sad too. Touch, touch me."[72] A man wants to connect through the physical, tying his feelings to everything around him with a touch. When he lies on the beach, smelling the salty sea air and feeling the warmth of the sun, he feels as if he's one with nature. When swims in a lake, lying back and floating on the water, he forgets where his body ends and the water begins.

When he makes love to a woman, he is one with her, body and soul. The sensual connection we all feel is an ever-present need and desire—an essential part of being human. It is fundamental to being a man, even if he doesn't speak a word. Intimate connection is what a man wants, and he robs himself of it by reducing sex to the physical—just a woman does when she looks at sex as anything other than her husband needing to be one with her.

## TO IGNORE OUR PHYSICAL NEEDS IS TO IGNORE THE NATURE OF OUR SEXUALITY.

The story of creation in the Bible is a powerful commentary on a man's sensual needs. Even though the first man had God for company, he needed someone fitting for him to help care for the world. God is pure spirit. Adam needed a companion who understood him as an equal, a physical entity to touch, hold, and know inside and out. Physicality was essential to ridding a man of loneliness. Should we be surprised then that a man feels most comforted and least alone when he is physically joined with a woman? Is it any wonder—aside from how good it feels—that he hungers for sexual intimacy? Is it any wonder that he is tempted to make a god of a woman's body—this beautiful form that makes him feel complete?

God formed woman from the cosmic man, taking the feminine within the first human and giving it physical form. One became two: the masculine form and the feminine made for each other, not just as spiritual and intellectual beings, but physical. To neglect this aspect of the marriage bond or to deride men for this need is to ignore how we are made. Many creation myths are a variation of this theme. The Zoroastrian creation myth portrays humanity as a plant that grew from a purified seed. This seed of the cosmic man was cleansed from all immorality and lies that had seeped into creation. It returned to the earth and became two stalks side by side—the first man and the first woman. This sensuality of nature is often lost to those who spiritualize humanity to the point of ignoring the physical needs. We put men and women together in close quarters—displaying their sexual glory whether they intend to or not—and we expect them to ignore their physical urges or to treat sensual desires as intrinsically evil, dangerous, or threatening when they are simply part of our identity.

Pro-feminist psychologists complain that men are too goal-oriented in sex—that they're simply about the orgasm. They say that "traditional masculinity" is fundamentally disconnected. In his book on reconstructing masculinity, Ronald Levant asserts, "Traditionally, men have separated sex from emotional intimacy. Lately, however, they've begun to rethink their beliefs about sex." Participants in Levant's studies said they were concerned about their sexual performance, but they "rejected the stereotypical 'male as stud, female as sex-object' ethic in favor of a more intimate, egalitarian, less goal-oriented approach to sex." The study participants said they rejected the "traditional notions" that "a man should always be ready for sex," that "hugging and kissing should always lead to intercourse," and that a man "shouldn't bother with sex unless he can achieve orgasm." They also rejected the idea "that men don't care who their sex partner is so long as she's willing." Instead, the men in Levant's study rejected traditional notions, asserting that "a man should love his sex partner."[73]

While I agree with the sentiments here, especially the last one, my problem with Levant's message here is he has cast "traditional masculinity" as the worst sorts of men. I was born in the '60s, and I never heard anyone telling men that "men are studs and women are sex objects," as if this is a tried-and-true "ethic." I heard it, but even then, it was considered deviant. Certainly, there have been machismo cultures in which sexual prowess is a measure of manhood, but these are not all, and they're not typical in the American experience, which has a varied and complex history regarding male sexuality. Levant would have you think that all men, until the last couple of decades, treated women as vehicles for their sexual release. This is not the case. Just read the letters of soldiers who fought in the Civil War. One is by Sullivan Ballou who served in the Federal army.

> Sarah, my love for you is deathless, it seems to bind me to you with mighty cables that nothing but Omnipotence could break.... The memories of the blissful moments I have spent with you come creeping over me, and I feel most gratified to God and to you that I have enjoyed them so long. And hard it is for me to give them up and burn to ashes the hopes of future years, when God willing, we might still have lived and loved together and seen our sons grow up to honorable manhood around us.[74]

This letter doesn't sound like a man who separated sex from emotional intimacy. It sounds like a man who adored his wife, honored her, and set her up on a pedestal of love. Levant speaks of wanting sex to be more "egalitarian," as if a woman's desires have never been considered until our post-sexual revolution enlightenment. What he fails to realize is that the high-powered men of the materialistic post-war 1950s did not define traditional masculinity then, before that time, or even now.

## TRADITIONAL MASCULINITY DOESN'T HAVE THE UGLY HISTORY FEMINISTS CLAIM.

In early America, women were "egalitarian" in more ways than reported today. Often, there were more women than men, which put women in the driver's seat when it came to mates. As documented in *America's Women* by Gail Collins, "Few women stayed single long in the South; some went through five or six husbands," often toying with men to find the best mate, promising to marry a suitor only to choose someone else. Men complained so much about this practice that Virginia passed a law prohibiting women from promising themselves to more than a single suitor (a glaring example of how a woman's freedom was restricted by the state).[75] Some women climbed socially with the death of each husband. Others were named executors of their former husbands' estates, and they refused to marry again because they didn't want to give up control of their property to a new husband.[76]

In the rough-and-tumble of the early colonies, there were cases of "women physically assaulting their enemies, turning their husbands out of their homes, leading religious dissent, and criticizing public officials to make it clear that there were plenty of female émigrés who knew what they wanted and weren't shy in making their feelings known."[77] In New England, "a third of the accused spouse beaters were women," and, when they went to court, women weren't punished as harshly as male abusers—though, when it came to adultery, women were killed, not the men (another glaring injustice that gave rise to later feminist movements).[78]

As for sex, the notion that traditional masculinity was all about the man just getting his orgasm with no concern about the woman's needs doesn't comport with a lot of our history. In early America, sex was enjoyed by both men and women—in marriage and out. From 1720 to 1740, about 10 percent of babies born were out of wedlock. From 1760 to 1780, that number jumped to 44 percent.[79] Premarital sex was fairly common and tolerated more often than we might think. The quality of sex was also of crucial importance. "Women were expected to enjoy sex," Collins writes. "Most people believed conception could occur only if a woman reached orgasm."[80] I wonder if some wise older woman spread that rumor for the benefit of ladies everywhere. Men read the sex book *Aristotle's Masterpiece* to learn how to please a woman—a required reading in some settings. Women made their expectations about sex clear, echoing ladies of today by saying, they "choose rather to have a thing done well than have it often."[81]

An interesting observation Collins makes about women throughout American history is that there was much more independence and equality during times of survival—when everyone needed all hands on deck and women had to toil next to the men, even in commerce. It has been during leisure times that women have focused more on their domestic spheres and receded into the more delicate Victorian frames of femininity. During times of necessity and survival, there was less selfishness, more service, less whining, and more discussion about how one's needs were getting met by the opposite sex. It is no surprise, then, that during the most leisure time in American history, the feminist movement burst forth. Besides the obvious need for legal equality in many areas of society, the notion that women were unhappy when they weren't doing the *same things* as men arose from bored housewives who had too much time on their hands.

Incidentally, it was during this leisure, economically focused period post-WWII that women began to objectify themselves. Within a materialistic frame, a woman's beauty and sexiness became her identity. Women's magazines burst onto the scene with tips about how to be beautiful. Diet became a verb for the first time in human history. Women were serving in the domestic sphere, but they had a lot of leisure time to pamper themselves and grow weary of the materialism of their lives. Their husbands came home and wanted sex, but bored wives felt disconnected from themselves and their purpose in life, so, naturally, they felt disconnected from their husbands. Men had their issues too, as competition focused on achieving and generating more income. But this wasn't the case everywhere in America. Not all men were high-powered achievers who treated their women as sex objects. Contrary to popular belief, not all men were New York executives like Don Draper, who used women to fulfill his own sexual needs and to plug the holes of his identity as a man and a human being.

Much of the intimacy and emotional connection of sexual relations in early America survived through the Gilded Age and the 1950s. I've talked to too many older women, including my mother, who wonder what these young feminists are talking about when they worry that loss of abortion rights will take them back to a sexual dystopia in which women were basically treated as sex slaves. "I don't recognize the world these women describe," my mother says. "Sure, we wanted more rights, but women were a lot more sexually empowered than these feminists assume."

My grandmother would laugh at such a notion of sexual slavery. While women weren't displaying their sexuality like they do today, and while they weren't publicly talking about their sexual exploits, women were generally satisfied with their husbands. Not all, but we can never say any generation is perfect because human beings aren't perfect. Most women, however, were content with their husbands. The idea that "traditional masculinity" as we've known it for most of American history is toxic and emotionally disconnected is not true to the facts.

In this book *Sex and the Eighteenth-Century Man*, Thomas Foster explains that marriage was a measure of adulthood for both men and women—and it was mostly a happy institution.

"Marriage brought emotional and financial stability, security and happiness," he writes. "Sexual intimacy was an important part of early American marriage. Colonial courts allowed divorces and separations due to sexual misconduct or sexual inability." Significantly, "husbands bore the brunt of responsibility for harmonious marital relations, including sexual relations."[82]

Having babies was only part of the importance of sex for Americans, from colonial times to present day—though that was important, especially for men. When we talk about measuring a man's masculinity by his "sexual prowess" today, we often think of it as how many women he beds. This was not "traditional masculinity." A man's masculine sexual identity was tied to his "sexual prowess" or virility, but that was measured by how many children he bore. Having children was a point of pride, and not because it showed that a man could have an orgasm and achieve his sexual conquest. It was a part of a masculine man's identity because having children was essential to being an adult who was responsible for someone else.

Being a man meant becoming a productive member of society—to make it better through good governance, invention, and godliness. Being a man was caring for others, meeting their needs, providing for them, and protecting them. Being a man was satisfying the wife in the bedroom. Traditional masculinity was inherently selfless. Marriage, not sexual liberty, shaped a boy into a man. Today, we have a society of boys—and women have contributed to that stunted maturity with their own sexual immaturity.

With its focus on democratic freedoms, marriage in America focused on mutual affection, love, and compatibility, not one's station in life—as it was in aristocratic Europe. Marriages were born of romantic love and commitment before God. This combination created a satisfying arrangement for both husbands and wives. Intimacy in sex was very much a part of that—and so was "goal-oriented" sex, in which the man's orgasm was necessary. Early American men never apologized for their powerful desires for sex and for the release that came from it. They saw no conflict between emotional connection and orgasm because they also understood how to connect with their wives. Marriage was a gift given to men and women, so they could express their passion freely within a trusted relationship in which love was the basis. A woman could give herself to her husband when he needed it, even when she didn't feel like it, because she loved him and she knew he loved her. A man could take his time and tend to the sexual needs of his wife while still wanting to reach the end of sex in that climactic moment because he loved her and he knew she loved him. They were both committed not only to each other, but to the purpose of sex as designed for procreation and intimacy within a covenantal relationship.

Recognition that men had aggressive sexual urges did not lead Americans to conclude that their masculinity was toxic. A man's sexuality was God-designed for a purpose. But a man's sexual desires did not define or rule over him. He was expected to exercise self-control. This was a mark of manhood. "In a message titled 'On Entrance into LIFE, and the Conduct of early MANHOOD,' reprinted in the *American Herald* in 1786," Foster writes, "Moderation and self-control were emphasized: 'You have violent passions implanted in you by nature for the accomplishment of her purposes. But conclude not, as many have done to their ruin, that because they are violent, they are irresistible. The same nature which gave you passions, gave you also reason and a love of order.'"[83] Marriage was a guard against so-called "toxic masculinity." Is it any wonder with the decline of marriage—or the delay of it—we have an increase of so-called toxic masculinity?

The message to men before the rampant materialism of the twentieth century, the real "traditional masculinity" that we have lost, was that "A Marriage entered into without mutual tenderness, is one kind of rape." This, from an article on the "Maxims of Love." It continues: "In marriage, prefer the person before wealth, virtue before beauty, and the mind before the body—then you have a WIFE, a FRIEND, and a COMPANION."[84] Sexual satisfaction was an important part of this relationship, for both men and women. Foster found "evidence from divorce records and other papers that reveal a masculine pride at being able to give pleasure to a woman. Here, the measure of sexual prowess was not simply based on the number of conquests or the ability to take and use a woman at will. Here, the power was based on pleasing a woman physically." Additionally, "deficient husbands" were "blamed for unsatisfied wives."[85]

This is not to say there wasn't abuse or unhappy marriages in those days. The records are replete with abusive husbands (and wives) and divorces due to unfaithfulness and cruelty. But these failures of masculinity were not praised as essential traits of masculinity or, as Levant puts it in his book on reconstructing masculinity, a masculine "ethic." Quite the contrary. Abusive men, neglectful men, and adulterers lost status in the community and risked their social positions. They had failed at their highest calling of manhood—caring for their wife and family. Interestingly, even when a woman strayed, the husband was considered a failure. Such is the cost of leadership within the home.

> Whether committed by the husband or the wife, infidelity ultimately signaled the failure of the husband to create and maintain an orderly, stable, and monogamous household. When husbands sought sexual relationships outside their marriages, they exhibited a lack of manly self-control. When wives engaged in extramarital relations, their betrayal challenged a man's position as head

> of household and showed him humiliated by her disrespect. His reputation would also have been challenged by the man with whom his wife had had the affair. In divorce testimony, both men and women not only complained of the disruption to household order that adultery causes but also used the language of lost love to express the emotional toll that was exacted.[86]

## THE SEXUAL REVOLUTION DRIVEN BY FEMINISM HAS PLAYED A ROLE IN CREATING "TOXIC MASCULINITY."

This commitment to love and sex within marriage didn't disappear in the nineteenth, twentieth, or twenty-first centuries. Traditional masculinity didn't ubiquitously morph into sexual disconnection and abuse. Yet something has happened to sex in America. Too many people are complaining about sexual dissatisfaction. Loneliness and emotional disconnection plague men and women who seek professional help to overcome the emptiness they feel. But is "toxic masculinity" the cause of these issues? Are men to blame? Do men need to change and become more feminized for everyone to be happier? Do men need to form more physical bonding groups with other men to find greater happiness? Do men need to detach from women as a source of emotional sharing and open themselves up to sharing with other men in more intimate ways to drive the loneliness from their souls?

The answers to these questions are complicated. Male companionship is essential to male happiness, and emotional expression is needed for any individual to thrive in a relationship. But I posit that the emotional disconnect and loneliness that psychologists say are plaguing men, in particular, will not be solved by reconstructing traditional masculinity. It will be by empowering it, rediscovering it where it has been lost, and recognizing the purpose of manhood in its own right and not as reflected by the feminine. Egalitarian sexuality is not the answer. Godly sexuality is.

Key to a man's healthy sexuality is to have a right understanding of sex and marriage. The loss of this understanding is at the root of the sex problem in America today. This means women need a right understanding of sex and marriage as well. What is the purpose of sex? Is it simply to gratify one's own lusts? Is it a mere physical exchange of fluids? Is it using another person a means to an end? Is it free sexual expression and autonomy? It's none of these things. Sex was designed by God in the context of love—and not just any love—the love between a man and woman in a committed relationship. That oneness is attained in the act of sex itself when two people are joined together, body and soul. It is also achieved when a child is produced from that union—the DNA of the man and woman literally becoming one in the creation of a new human being. Having a child is the ultimate act of creation and one of the most honorable and glorious ways we live out God's image on earth.

The problem with women and the sexual revolution is that they began to think of sex and sexuality as separate from a relationship with a man. That sounds weird, I know. We are talking about sex, after all. But it has become an individualistic act, even if another body is present. Feminism has taught us that a woman's body is hers to do with as she wills, whether it's stripping naked, doing porn, sleeping with several men, or killing the baby in her womb that's the product of her free choice to have sex. While a woman is certainly free from any government intrusion to express her sexuality, she is not free from her moral obligations as a human being and as a female who was designed for a purpose by God. Neither is a man. We are, as created human beings, bound by the purposes of our Creator—to live according to his righteous will as we seek responsible dominion of the earth through empathy, and to love others. That empathy is not just emotional or active, but spiritual as we are always aware that human beings are not tools to use as we wish, but spiritual creatures made in God's image to be loved as an end unto themselves.

Sex is an essential part of our purpose as men and women—it is intensely relational, unifying, and designed for connection and love. This joining of the masculine and feminine is a beautiful expression of completion. It's where we find our full humanity. Sex in a loving, covenantal relationship is the physical expression of God's communal design for humanity. We are not meant to be alone. The feminine is not meant to be separate from the masculine. Men and women are designed to be one. This is the essence of marriage.

## We need to learn more about the "why" of sex, not the "how."

If both husbands and wives looked at sex not as something to get, but something to give as a means of connection and completion, they would have fewer conflicts about sex. If they trusted the foundation of love for each other, they wouldn't be so defensive in the bedroom. Many books are written about the practicalities of sex—techniques, tips on how to please your spouse, advice to men on how to please a woman, and vice versa. I'm not going to focus on the "hows" of sex. Instead, I want you to think about what sex is, its purpose, and why you are doing it. A right understanding of the true meaning of sex will go a long way in fixing a lot of practical problems regarding a couple's sex life. Once you understand the purpose, you can explore many ways to enjoy it together. Every couple's sexual relationship will be different, and it is not anyone's business to impose the how-tos on others. But the "why" of sex is foundational for us all. When we understand that, everything else begins to fall in place. And in that space is a lot of freedom—and fun.

Foundational to understanding the purpose of sex is to see that it is designed to be between a man and a woman, the *physical* and *spiritual* completion of the feminine and masculine. Our bodies are not separated from our spirits. A woman's body Is designed to be joined with a man's, and vice versa. The very act of procreation screams this reality. But there's more to the design of sex than making babies. There is a wholeness that is created in the physical joining. God fashioned the woman to be the perfect companion to the man. Her body, mind, heart, soul—all are an ideal complement to him, as he is to her. When two people fall in love and marry, committing themselves to each other in a trusting relationship, the purpose of sex unfolds naturally—as long as both of them understand that the purpose of sex is not for personal gratification (though it is intensely personally gratifying). It is designed for social completion. It is "other-centered," not "me-centered."

Sex is the act of two distinct entities—male and female—coming together as a whole. They are the two halves of human existence. It is damaging to the sexual relationship, therefore, to expect the other to be exactly like you. The man is not the woman, and the woman is not the man. The masculine and feminine are different—polar opposites—that are attracted to each other because of those differences. The feminine is drawn to the masculine like a magnet, and the energy that is released in that attraction is the stuff of poetry, passion, and perpetual turbulence in the human experience.

Unfortunately, too many women expect men to be like women when it comes to sex. Instead of seeing his differences and letting him be a man, she wants him to act in a more familiar frame. "If only my husband would talk to me more before we have sex!" As

I've written above, men express with their actions and, when it comes to sex, they want a lot more action and a little less talk. Men have their unjustified complaints too. "I wish my wife would strip down and get to it without all the foreplay. Sometimes I just want to have sex!" Well, women aren't men. They need more emotional connection on the front end. Men get their emotional release from the very act of sex. Women need an emotional release to have sex. It's the same way with how men and women communicate. Men say what they mean, and they expect women to discern the feelings behind what they say. Women say what they feel, and they expect men to figure out what they actually mean. If we aren't aware of how the other communicates both in words and sex, we will be forever frustrated.

So what do we do with these opposites and sex? The answer is love built on trust. It's the bridge between these two "warring" identities. When a woman is in love with her husband, she thinks of him and doesn't try to refashion him in her image. Love means she has sex with him after a long day of taking care of the kids or working in the office—even when she isn't in the mood. Love means she takes care of herself and looks feminine and sexy because men are attracted visually. No man wants to come home to a frumpy wife. Love means that she tells him what she wants sexually and doesn't expect him to read her mind. It means she recognizes that sex itself is her husband connecting with her, and she doesn't need him to spill his emotions before every sexual encounter. It means that sometimes her husband needs sex with her to release his pent-up emotions. Sex relaxes him, making him able and willing to express his feelings—maybe not immediately afterward, but certainly in general. It also means having sex even when you're both angry at each other. Sometimes sex is the best bandage to heal wounds. We call it "make-up" sex, but sometimes having sex can lead to making up because you connect at a deeper level and are reminded that the two of you are one. In sex, you both become vulnerable and anger dissipates.

When a woman is showing love, being aware of what a man needs in sex and how he emotes, the man should be doing the same. When a man loves his wife, he thinks of her and doesn't try to refashion her in his own image—or worse, the image of other women, a problem created by pornography (which I'll discuss in Chapter 8). This means he senses when she needs to talk and listens to her express her emotions, even if he doesn't understand them. It means he takes his time while making love, giving her the foreplay she needs to enjoy sex as much as he does. It means taking care of her sexual needs before he gets his met. It means holding her afterward, not falling asleep as if she were just a receptacle for his sexual energy.

When both are thinking of the other person and when expectations are cast aside, love blossoms and a healthy sexual relationship is the result. This dynamic will not be steady, of course. We're human. Sometimes the man is too tired to talk and wants to have sex with his wife and find comfort and release in her arms. He's not going to be as thoughtful as he needs to be. Sometimes a woman is too tired working all day, and the last thing she wants is sex. Both should be respectful of the others' needs at these times. If this behavior becomes the norm, then you have a problem. But, when you both are working on loving the other, you will forgive these times. Sometimes, they might last for a season (especially if health issues are involved), but you show each other grace because the foundation of your sex life is love.

## Egalitarian sex is a myth.

Showing grace should be extended to people outside the marriage relationship as well. Most of the complaining we hear about "toxic masculinity" isn't in marriage, but in the rest of society where men and women interact every day. A problem with the "egalitarian" sexuality that pro-feminist activists and psychologists advocate is that it is pushing for a kind of equality that goes beyond rights and respect of others. It is a blending of the feminine and the masculine into an androgynous form in which sex is irrelevant. The feminist movement has been pushing for women to be more masculine for decades, making modern feminism an attack on femininity as much as masculinity. Women have been pressured to leave the domestic sphere and enter the workplace where they compete with men and with one another. The mantra has been, "Women can do anything a man does." In many areas of performance, this is true. Given education and training, women certainly can succeed as well as men in most professional arenas. But this doesn't change who they essentially are as females—and it doesn't negate their sexuality or how men perceive it.

Healing must come through reestablishment of trust between the sexes, and that can't happen as long as men are considered sexual threats just for being masculine. Are men driven by their sexual urges? Yes, of course. But are all men dogs? Despite their impulses, needs, and desires, I'd say most—by and large—are not. Think of the billions of respectful interactions men and women that happen every day. If you listened only to feminists, you'd think women were being raped on every street corner. It's just not happening that frequently.

My problem with a lot of the messaging to "tame" men these days is that it is an attempt to deny their fundamental nature as men. The truth is, healthy women don't want that. They want a man to be sexually attracted to them (especially if the man is attractive—let's be honest about that). They want both men and women to exercise their sexual freedoms responsibly. They want both men and women to grow up. They want men who desire them, who will fight for them, and who will sweep them into their arms and kiss them deeply. They want to be put on a pedestal, not brought down as an "equal" to a man. Healthy women love the sexual dynamic between men and women. When that dynamic is treated with maturity and respect, relationships flourish.

The man in the office who thinks his coworker is beautiful and tells her so isn't demeaning her; he's admiring feminine beauty. As one man said, "Just because I like your boobs, doesn't mean I want to rape you. It doesn't even mean that I want to have sex with you—though, not many men turn down an offer of sex. It's how we're made." And you know what? That's okay, though I wouldn't recommend going around telling female coworkers that you like their boobs. That's not the point of the comment above. The point is that men are sexual beings and notice women's bodies. It's fine that men think about sex and want to have sex. They're designed to procreate, to woo the beauty, and to delight in her body. They're sensual. To change that is to change their masculine identity.

For a materialistic society, America often becomes rather anti-physical when it comes to pushing a feminist agenda. They'll applaud a woman displaying her physical form any way she wants, but they condemn a man who responds to that physical form. They expect men to become dualistic, treating their physical needs and desires as somehow evil and elevating the mind to the ultimate good. This is nonsensical. As men and as women, we are both physical and spiritual. To remain healthy, we can't become physically reductionistic or spiritually reductionistic. Ironically, some feminists act like stereotypical Puritans of old when they deny the sexual nature of a man and expect him to live in denial of it—and, worse, to be ashamed of it.

Men want women to give them a break when it comes to sex. Accept them as they are. Expect them to be mature and certainly challenge them when they're not, but don't reduce them to a disembodied eunuch who doesn't feel fire in his loins when encountering the glory of feminine sexuality. Let him be who he is, feel what he feels, need what he needs, and love him for it.

## CHAPTER 8

# MASCULINITY INTERRUPTED

*Go back to Socrates: "Know thyself." For Socrates, there are only two kinds of people: the wise, who know they are fools; and fools, who think they are wise. Similarly, for Christ and all the prophets, there are only two kinds of people: saints, who know they are sinners; and sinners, who think they are saints. Which are you?*

—Peter Kreeft

When I first started writing this book, I decided I would not get into the negatives of how men can act. That wasn't my purpose. My goal was to celebrate masculinity, not poke holes in it. We hear criticism of men daily in the media, television, films, and the education system. "Men are dogs" is a common refrain, and I didn't want to add to it. Masculinity is under attack, and I wanted to bring some balance to the debate by discussing how masculinity is not toxic. I wanted to help women better understand their relationships with men and appreciate masculinity and in all its glory.

However, as I delved into the pages of my book, I began to realize that a good warning is never a bad thing. The fact is that men aren't always good, just as some men who are good aren't always masculine. Some men fall short of the ideals of masculinity, and some deserve the anger and distrust they have received from women in their lives.

My purpose in showing how some men fail to achieve mature masculinity is not to beat up men in general or defame masculinity itself. It is to encourage men to see their own shortcomings and women to understand that these deviancies are not masculinity as it should be but masculinity in an undeveloped and corrupted state. I don't even like to refer to these behaviors as masculine. They are simply bad character, which can be seen among women as well. The man who is abusive because he is deeply insecure with a bloated sense of ego is just like the woman who lashes out at those around her because she has allowed pride and fear to fashion her sense of self. The woman who sleeps around with every stranger she meets is no different from the man who uses one woman after another to fill the emptiness inside of him, born not of hatred for others but a warped view that other people are a means to an end. They both continually search for someone new to revitalize their deadened souls, and both are failing to act according to their purpose as designed by God—to serve and love others.

## WHEN MEN FAIL AS LOVERS, THE HEART IS BROKEN AND THE SOUL LOST.

The next morning, I knew I had been used. For weeks, the guy I'd developed a crush on in class had been sending me notes, leaving cards at my door, and sending me little tokens of affection—a poem, flowers, my favorite wine cooler (back in the Bartles &

Jaymes days). I fell for the romance and gave myself to him one night in a hotel room. It was passionate, everything I'd hoped it would be. Afterward, he slipped away sometime in the night. It could have been a scene from any love story with a bad ending. I only wish I'd seen the warning signs.

When I tracked him down later that day, the dead look in his eyes told me everything: detachment, disconnection, and despondency. He was far away—nothing like the man who had seduced me with poetry and promises of love. He was nice enough. He promised to give me a call—next week, maybe. I walked away, humiliated and angry at myself for being fooled—and ashamed that I had let lust get the better of me. I'd fallen for the immature lover, the man who used women for his own satisfaction and discarded them as easily. I've seen it time and again throughout my life in many different ways, either personally or through the tears of friends and colleagues who suffered the same.

When I was an advertising executive for a newspaper, I walked into the office of a client, a used car salesman who often flirted with me. I sat down at his desk, and he got up to close the door. On the way back, he stood behind me. As I started to turn to ask him what he was doing, I felt his hands on my shoulders. I don't even remember what he said. All I was conscious of was his hands moving down toward my breasts. I got up quickly and left, later passing off the account to one of my male colleagues. I never told anyone. He was just one more man who didn't understand the purpose of his sexuality, of being a lover—that sex was meant to be in the context of commitment and covenant. Erotic love is designed to make a man and woman one—body and soul. It is to be born out of service, selflessness, and adoration. It's not a mere vehicle for selfish pleasure or a means to tap into a fleeting feeling or a desperate grasp for something to make you feel alive.

### The sex industry is one of the most prevalent evils in today's society.

One of the most common forms of men using women is through pornography (though women have jumped on the porn-watching bandwagon these days as well). Pornography deadens the heart like nothing else, as people celebrate it in the name of mutual consent and liberty. But free agency doesn't determine or negate morality, and it doesn't change the needs of the human heart. I understand that some men turn to pornography or prostitution because they've been hurt in relationships, used and abused by women to the point that they'd prefer a financial transaction or an online hook-up to a marriage contract. It's easier. It's free of risk. But it's also harmful. It hurts those we say we love, it hurts those we don't even know, and it hurts us.

Imagine a college girl getting ready for a date. She has always been insecure when it comes to sex, but she finally decided to go through with it. She touches up her makeup, styles her hair, picks out a dress showing just the right amount of skin—at least, she thinks so. She's excited but nervous. She hopes he isn't disappointed with her. She likes him and wants their relationship to last. Little does she know that she's only one in a long line of girls he has seduced. He watches porn daily and has sex often, though lately he's found it difficult to get excited. Sex isn't as intense as it used to be, so he tries one girl after another, looking for something new to stimulate him. He doesn't want to seem like a user. He likes, even loves, each girl—that's what he tells himself and them. They're all sexy in their own way, but one is never enough. He longs for more to soothe the ache inside, the hunger that is never satisfied. Late at night, he's lonely, so he turns on porn, trying to fill the emptiness no real girl can fill. But it doesn't last. Nothing does. He's always searching.

Imagine a wife lying in bed, waiting for her husband to come upstairs. She slips into the simple cotton lingerie she bought that day—just the kind he likes. They both have been busy with work and the kids that intimate time together has passed too often. She misses him, the feel of him against her, the passion of his kisses as he looks into her eyes. She waits, having hinted an hour ago that she was ready. Still, he doesn't come. This isn't the first time he has been late. It seems his interest has waned or, when he has wanted her, he's rushed. He hasn't been quite himself—not as tender, not as connected. She leaves the bedroom and goes to his office door. It's closed. She opens it without knocking only to find him looking at a photo of a naked woman on the computer screen. It's not distasteful—just a picture of a woman online in thigh-high lace stockings with perky breasts and flirty eyes. Her husband turns, but his wife is already gone. He's a little embarrassed, but not much. It's just a picture. It doesn't mean anything. He goes to the bedroom to soothe her. Instead of pouting and turning away, she makes love to him, desperately trying to be what he wants, to feel that connection she once felt, to make him *see* her again—all the while self-conscious of her sagging breasts against his chest. Her body will never be the same—not after five children. She squeezes her eyes to fight back the tears.

Imagine a woman standing in front of a camera. She sets the lights just right, her skin glowing, her body toned. She arches her back to show her naked breasts as she tosses her long hair across her shoulder. She snaps the picture and sends it to one of her fans. She takes a couple more and adds them to the pile of images she has collected for years. They're her legacy, her claim to her own body and her freedom from the control of others. She's had a hard life—emotional struggles, sexual abuse, devastating breakups. To take the reins of her own life, she decided to do porn, though she doesn't like to call it that. It's just nude pictures. It's how she expresses herself. "There's no harm in it."

Never does she consider the man's wife. She assumes she doesn't bear any responsibility for the woman's pain—at least, that's what she tells herself. She's just providing a service, like a dealer selling drugs. Payment and lack of personal involvement somehow erase the morality and social responsibility of the exchange. When she looks into the camera, she believes she's merely expressing her authenticity and sharing herself with others—a free spirit. But it's the exact opposite. The photos are one-dimensional copies of a single aspect of her being. Her spirit is caged by the image. Her body is meant for connection, and her eyes are designed to look into those of another—a man who knows her in real life and loves her imperfections. But there is no one looking back at her when the camera clicks. There's no connection in the cold, empty eyes of a lens. All she feels is a shiver in the heat of the lights and a momentary thrill that a man out there is excited to see her naked body.

Inside her is the little girl who struggled with body issues, still feeling small and insignificant, a sad whimper in her soul. For years, she has tried to silence the whispered cries by taking control of her body and putting it out there for the affirmation and approval of others, recreating herself in a thousand different ways. The more they applaud, the more she wants and needs it. The attention exhilarates her like a drug. It makes her feel like she's in complete control of herself and her destiny. It makes her feel known. But she isn't in control. The others are. She isn't known. Only her body, captured in a moment, is seen. Her self-esteem is built on outward projections, on subjective affirmations of others, instead of the objective reality of who she truly is as a fully integrated human being whose worth is established by her Maker. His purposes—his adoration and love—could be her island, solid and secure in a world spinning out of control. Instead, she is adrift on the tides that shift and change with the wind.

When the voices go silent and the camera is off, when the lights are out, she's alone. She feels detached, isolated—even from herself. No one gives her what she needs—the worth that can come only from within as the soul touches the divine. For so long, she has thought only of herself. Her needs. Her liberty. Her feelings. She has failed to show empathy to others, to wives, to men, to other young women who can't measure up to an idealized nude photo or erase those images from the minds of the men they love. Mostly, she has failed to show empathy to the woman looking at her from the mirror.

She thinks she found herself before the camera, but that's where she lost herself. Others know her body—at least, as she presents it in a single frame, but they don't know her. They can't. She doesn't even know herself. Her only real hope, as it is with all people, is to find connection, meaning, and desire in relationships that matter, beginning with the One who knows them best. They can then carry that knowledge, that light of love, into every other relationship and watch them flourish like petals spreading at dawn. Or they can cast it aside for a passing feeling that disappears into darkness.

## Sexual neglect is a failure of masculinity.

The failure of a man to be a lover as God designed him to be is not relegated to sex addicts and rakes. The man who is a weakling at loving, who is so detached that he doesn't try to connect sexually, even with his wife, has failed to live up to his calling as a masculine lover. Some men never grow up and shed the need for their mother's approval. They are so used to seeing women as a mother figure that a woman as a powerful, alluring, sexual creature is intimidating.

These men often enjoy their wives as mothers of their children, but they don't know what to do with them as vixens in the bedroom.

I have heard from too many women in sexless marriages who wonder what is wrong with their husbands. Many of these men—like those who are driven to be Don Juans and Don Drapers with their sexual exploits—are more in love with pornography than the women in their lives. Instead of putting in the work of loving a flesh-and-blood woman, they sit in front of a screen and get off watching porn. The supply is endless—always something new to titillate. But it doesn't last; it doesn't satisfy. They're eating Turkish delight, but it evaporates in their stomachs—leaving them hungrier than when they started. "The less a guy feels like a real man in the presence of a real woman, the more vulnerable he is to porn," John Eldredge rightly says in *Wild at Heart*.[87]

The explosion of pornography in America has a lot of causes—access being the main one. But I think a more deep-seated reason is that men don't know how to relate to women today, and so they turn to porn for satisfaction. I have seen this among men who have turned their back on intimate relationships with women because they have suffered under the "tyranny" of feminism in their personal lives. Many are enamored with pornography, so much so that, when I criticize it, they shut me out, no matter how much of an advocate of men I am. Pornography has become their outlet and their idol, as they have lost the ability and desire to interact with real women. They don't know how to engage with women anymore, so they give up and turn to fantasy. Too many women in the porn industry are willing to indulge them. The spiral into darkness is hard to stop. "A man's heart, driven into the darker regions of the soul, denied the very things he most deeply desires, comes out in darker places," Eldredge observed.[88]

I've found this to be true. Men I know, who are avid watchers of pornography, have a coldness about them that I don't see in other men. They have disconnected themselves from their purpose as masculine lovers and have resorted to using women as tools for their selfish ends. The result is profound loneliness they keep trying to chase away with porn and more porn. The men who have completely detached themselves from women (even those who are still married) find their sexual expression only in the darkness of porn. Men who are addicted to sex, those who are always in search of someone new to "connect with," watch porn but continue to prowl for women to bed with images of porn actresses dancing in their heads. Some are even self-deceived enough to think they love the women they've seduced. These are the most deceptive types. They seem so earnest and sincere in their flirtations. They connect with words and lure women into their trap because they believe their own machinations. They think they're loving and giving to the woman, even going so far as to think they're doing what's best for her. But, after they've bedded her and drained her of the only thing they were searching for, she's discarded because she doesn't satisfy.

## Women need to see the immature lover as he is, not as she imagines him to be.

Part of a woman's responsibility in the erotic dance between men and women is to discern the intentions of men. Too many women today don't see the immature lover for who he is. A woman believes the man who is disconnected sexually is merely self-controlled and respectful, and that her desire for sex is somehow misplaced. This sexual neglect occurs a lot in religious circles. She doesn't see that he's uncomfortable with her feminine sexuality, doesn't know what to do with it, and might secretly resent her as a lover. A physically healthy married man who is a good person, but who is not interested in fulfilling his responsibilities as a lover, is not living as

God intended. Neither is the wife when she denies her husband sexual intimacy.

The marriage relationship changes as the couple ages, of course, and health issues can interrupt sex. But there is a depth of sexual intimacy that can still be experienced that doesn't involve intercourse. When this is denied in a relationship between two healthy adults, the marriage has changed. A covenantal relationship that is supposed to be based on physical and spiritual oneness has transformed from erotic to platonic. The two have become merely friends—a good thing in its own right, but not the quality of marriage God designed.

On the other end of the spectrum, too many women fail to see that the man who sleeps around isn't the man they want long term. He becomes easily bored. He often has other women on the side, is incapable of being faithful, and hasn't learned to connect with a woman in a trusting relationship. With the feminist movement pushing women to imitate immature men and their dog-like ways, women are feeding the very pathologies they criticize. They are sleeping around, making sex easy, and putting themselves out there to be used. Then they're surprised when men treat them as tools and mere puppets in their pornographic plays.

Mature masculine lovers see sex in its right frame—as a means to bring two people together as a whole. It is not just about making babies, but about bringing together the two sides of human nature—both made in the image of God—and transforming it into glorious completion. It's about companionship that is more intimate than friendship. It's about oneness—the cure to loneliness. As old-fashioned as it might sound, sex in marriage is the best sex because it is sex as intended. It's where trust is formed, love is nurtured, and another soul is known. It's where God's image shines most brightly and where Christ's love for his church in emulated.

## WHEN A MAN FAILS TO BE THE KING GOD INTENDED, HE BECOMES A TYRANT OR A WEAKLING.

The King archetype for men is one of the most powerful, as a man in leadership exercises control in his particular sphere to bring order to chaos and well-being to those in his care. Literature is replete with stories of kings who have led their people well, fathers who have served their families, and leaders who have been good stewards of this earth. King Arthur of Camelot is a shining ideal of a king who sought the good of his people. Aragorn of *The Lord of the Rings* brought healing to his country by fighting evil in the face of impossible odds. King David in the Bible—even with his faults—was a man after God's own heart, who built a nation devoted to the Lord and established a beacon of light in this world that shines through the ages.

I've experienced in my own life a man I'm proud to call king of our home. I've often mentioned on social media how I love to cook for him and help him. It has become a playful joke for me to post pictures on Twitter of beer I serve him. The blowback I've received from feminists for this simple display of love is shocking, but it speaks to the hardness of women's hearts against men. I don't let the naysayers deter me. I won't let modern feminism with its pathologies rob me of enjoyment of my king. He cares for our family, working long hours and always hurrying home to be with those he loves. He serves us more than we serve him. He sacrifices for us more than we sacrifice for him. He shows me abundant grace when I don't deserve it, bringing order to my chaotic inner world. When I'm sick, he's by my side. When I've been emotionally traumatized, he has stood by me. When I've sinned against him, he has forgiven me, inspiring me to be better. He has challenged the children to be the best they can be, and he has done it with strength and gentleness. When he travels for business, he can't wait to get home because I treat him like a king and not an extra body that merely brings home a paycheck.

Not all fathers, husbands, and leaders in the community are like this. Abuse abounds. Fathers are cruel to their children. Husbands abuse their wives. We see government leaders in our nation lording over us because they long for power instead of serving those who have voted them into office. These are immature men (and women), little tyrants who exploit and abuse rather than help others. Our society is guilty of putting tyrants into power because we are dazzled by their personalities or their weak promises instead of judging them by right standards. We perpetuate weak-minded men by giving them more authority instead of holding them to account for their selfishness. The tyrant only remains the tyrant as long as the people allow it. The people allow it because they have lost their way, putting their hope in men instead of God. They rally around man-made delusions and fantasies instead of relying on the objective realities of life and truth. As George R.R. Martin writes in *Fire and Blood*, "When the gods are silent, lords and kings will make themselves heard."[89]

The tyrant is only one abuse of the immature man. There is also the weakling who is paranoid about power and always suspect of others. He's deceptive, devious, and sometimes passive-aggressive. He wants to be king of his home, but he isn't willing to do the hard work of a king. Or, if he does the hard work, he whines when he doesn't get the appreciation he deserves. He wants those in his care to respect him and when he doesn't get it, he throws a temper tantrum, gets angry, or runs away, licking his wounds. While good men deserve respect, they don't always get it. The mature man doesn't whine about it, nor does he stop serving because he fails to get the return on investment he expects. He does his duty because that is his responsibility before God, and it doesn't change because it's not appreciated.

The weakling can be just as abusive as the tyrant, but he does it in a more roundabout way. He punishes through backstabbing and subtle cruelties. I had a friend whose father was a weakling like this. He would mock her at every turn and then complain that she disrespected him. She was always walking on eggshells, not knowing when he would be offended by something she or her mother would do or say. He would give her gifts but demand she use them as he wished. He never let her forget how hard he worked and how much he did for her, as if he were the victim of some great injustice and needed the affirmation of his subjects to prop up his ego. In just about every way, he saw himself as the one to be served, not as the one to serve. It crushed my friend, as she was weighed down with the burden of validating a man who could not be validated by his daughter. Because she always failed to do the impossible, he lived in a constant state of paranoia that no one loved him. That no one appreciated him. That no one understood him.

When I talk about men being kings, the feminists scoff, of course. "Why should men be so privileged?" they ask. But is it a privilege? Or is it a grave and serious responsibility—one, to be honest, I'd rather not have if I don't have to? To be a king is ultimately to be a servant. A husband is to love his wife as Christ loved the church—and Christ sacrificed his life for the church. To lead and rule is to take on all the hardships without complaint, to suffer the sins of others, and to pick up the pieces of others' failings. This doesn't mean a man becomes a doormat. Women have their responsibility to love their husbands (this whole book has been about that), but, if we're always waiting to serve until we get the appreciation we want, we become paralyzed. We become weak.

Bringing order to chaos is no easy task. It takes wisdom, self-control, knowledge, and love for others. Order is intrinsically other-centered. The king is using his power and gifts for the benefit of the kingdom. He is sacrificing himself so others can be provided for and protected. He is investing himself so that the seeds he has sown will thrive. If he suffers, he suffers in silence because others depend on him. If they're ungrateful, he continues to serve because this is his calling and his purpose. He doesn't toil because he will get the praise of those around him. He toils because he loves them.

The ultimate mark of a good leader and a noble king—the quality of a masculine man—is that he does what is right. The man who is abusive, cruel, and takes advantage of those under his care is not doing what is right. He is acting according to his lusts, wants, desires, and needs. The result is chaos. To do what is right is to bring order. The masculine man who is a leader in his home, over a nation, in the workplace, or in a church is, first and foremost, a man who exemplifies what is good, true, and righteous. The problem we face today is that we have discarded a sense of right and wrong. We cannot have masculine men fulfilling their calling as kings if we have abandoned objective truth. A culture of moral relativism is one rocked by forces of power vying for dominance. The tyrant and the weakling tear others apart to reconstruct them for his own purposes in a battle between subjective truths and realities. He makes his will the standard for all.

The role of the king is to lead others in "the way" of life, what C. S. Lewis called the Tao, borrowing from Eastern philosophy. The road the king leads others to follow is the fundamental truths of life and existence. "It is the doctrine of objective value, the belief that certain attitudes are really true, and others really false, to the kind of thing the universe is and the kind of things we are," Lewis writes in *The Abolition of Man*. "Those who know the Tao can hold that to call children delightful or old men venerable is not simply to record a psychological fact about our own parental or filial emotions at the moment, but to recognize a quality which demands a certain response from us whether we make it or not."[90]

A leader recognizes that there is intrinsic value and quality to life and people. We are not merely a collection of feelings, wishful thinking, and psychological processes. We are rooted in something real and objective, designed with a purpose. This understanding of human nature is the foundation of this book. Masculinity and femininity, while expressed in different ways by billions of people, are rooted in universals that stem from the very nature of God—the source of all existence. If this reality is not understood or embraced, then we are destined to live according to the whims of men and subject to their ever-changing desires in a game of power.

Without objective value and truth—without order to rule the chaos—we are merely bits of clay to be shaped and molded by others. As Lewis said,

> Either we are rational spirit obliged for ever to obey the absolute values of the Tao, or else we are mere nature to be kneaded and cut into new shapes for the pleasures of masters who must, by hypothesis, have no motive but their own "natural" impulses. Only the Tao provides a common human law of action which can over-arch rulers and ruled alike. A dogmatic belief in objective value is necessary to the very idea of a rule which is not tyranny or an obedience which is not slavery.[91]

The man who has not matured into his masculinity and who is either a tyrant or a weakling is a man ruled by denial of objective values and the responsibilities they require. He has set himself up as the pinnacle of truth, and he demands others bow to it. The mature masculine man sees himself and others in the context of

God's design, not his selfish purposes. He sees his wife as a complement to him, of equal value and worth, to be loved, protected, provided for, and covered by his strength. He respects her power as an influencer in his life and listens to her. The mature masculine man doesn't see his wife's gentle challenges or insights as threats, but he sees them as necessities for him to live well. When she explains the feelings of the children or their needs, she is fulfilling her role as his complement. He doesn't always see what she sees. He doesn't have her sensitivities or insights. He needs her to inform him and influence him without manipulation. When he is open to her wisdom and strength, he honors her as God made her. He doesn't reject her as a subservient, an irritant, or a nag. He loves her, embraces her, and respects her objective value that has nothing to do with his feelings or desires.

The mature masculine man looks at his children as creatures of great worth entrusted to his care. They are designed by God for divine purposes—they're not tools to be controlled and twisted by a father who can't see past his selfish feelings. The immature man looks at children and sees them as figures to be molded according to his will and pleasure. He wants his son to be an artist just like he is, not the athlete God made him to be, or vice versa. He demands that his daughter reflect an image he wants for her, not the unique creation she is—designed by God, for his divine purposes, not a man's.

Just as bad is the weakling man who lets his children grow untended and untrained. Instead of tending to the garden of his home, he allows the weeds grow wild. Children are given to parents to nurture as God intended, but parents who think they are enlightened let children "be what they are" and take no steps to intervene and direct them onto the right path. This might seem contradictory to what I said before—that fathers are to raise their children as God made them. Indeed, they are. Children are to be raised according to God's design for them as human beings as well as individuals, not according to the purposes and selfish desires of a father. This means a father should respect who the child is separate from himself but also respect that the child is never separate from God.

The mature father knows what God wants of the child and imparts that training and wisdom to the child. The job of the father is to train children to look to the source of their identity to know themselves, and that source is not the child himself or the parents who made him. Neither is it the state, the education system, a cabal of psychologists, or their friends. Our identity is determined by an objective source—by God. Even if you don't believe in a personal God, it is logical to see that objective truth regarding human nature is necessary for order. Without it, there is only chaos. Without it, there is no love, only power. As George Orwell put it, "Power is in tearing human minds to pieces and putting them together again in new shapes of your own choosing."[92]

## A MAN WHO USES HIS POWER FOR EVIL HAS BECOME A MONSTER.

Let's be honest, a man's strength is scary. By nature, he is dangerous—in his physical form alone. If aggression were all there was to a man—only sheer power—he'd be a villain. He'd be Big Brother in Orwell's *1984*, Patrick Bateman in *American Psycho*, The Republic of Gilead in *The Handmaid's Tale*, or Darth Vader in *Star Wars*. The list is endless, as is our fascination with fictional villains. They remind us of human nature twisted by love of power instead of motivated by love of people. Sadly, we see it too often. Our prisons are filled with men who can't control their aggression. They've given themselves over to depravity and lost control. Young men, frustrated, misguided, or driven by a corrupt mind, gun down innocent children in schools. Criminals wreak havoc on peaceful communities as they rob people on the streets, rape women, and kill without a thought. Terrorists bomb innocents in the name of religion, fueled by anger and dogma that devalues fellow human beings.

On September 11, 2001, evil men hijacked planes and flew them into the Twin Towers in New York and the Pentagon in Washington, D.C, killing and injuring thousands. In the skies above Pennsylvania, they took over Flight 93, aiming for the Capitol or the White House. In that moment of horror, there was a convergence of men at their best and their worst. As the terrorists flew toward their targets, the passengers in the back of the plane hatched a plan to bring them down. "I know we're all going to die," Thomas Burnett Jr. told his wife over his cell phone. "There's three of us who are going to do something about it. I love you, honey." The passengers had learned that the plane was heading to Washington to be used as a weapon, and they weren't going to let that happen. As they huddled together with phone lines open, one of the male passengers, Todd Beamer, was heard saying, "Are you guys ready? Let's roll." Led by brave men, the passengers attacked. The hijackers responded by rolling the plane to disrupt the charge. In the chaos, they lost control of the plane. It rolled onto its back and crashed into a field in Shanksville, Pennsylvania to the chants of "Allah is great." Both men and women were heroes that day as they faced evil. They countered toxic aggression at its worst with bravery, and they saved lives even as they lost their own.

## Feminism has both degraded women and weakened men.

While the sadist spreads cruelty, it is not the only kind of abuse. Some men use their aggression for evil, but some do nothing. They are cowards. As wise men have said, "All that is necessary for the triumph of evil is for good men to do nothing." I see this in some of the men's movements that have abandoned any sense of responsibility to women. They refuse to defend them. I even heard one man tell his son that if he sees a woman lying in the street alone at night to leave her there, that it's not worth the false accusations or lawsuits that could result from helping her. Such bitter cowardice is not masculinity. This is a man who has allowed feminine abuse, criticism, oppression, and his own failures to corrupt his manhood. He has become a coward.

Feminism, with its constant attack on masculinity, is helping to create not only sadists who are reacting to disrespect and rejection fostered by movements that elevate women over men, but weaklings who are turning their backs on their purpose to defend the weak. While it's a man's choice to act this way and he's responsible for his lack of action, we would be fools to ignore that this behavior has been fueled, at least in part, by modern feminism.

I see this detachment among men who are sick and tired of women believing they're equal to men in every way, even physically. Feminists are pushing women to be on the front lines in the military. Because military leaders made this possible, women are now at risk of having to sign up for selective service. Legally and constitutionally, once our government said women could serve equally to men in combat, the exception of women being "drafted" has been made null and void. To continue to draft only men is a constitutional violation of equal treatment. Men's groups, even now, are fighting in the courts to remove the exception and force girls to sign up with the boys.

This is valid on the legal front, but I have a serious problem with this on the ethical front and in light of our purposes and obligations as men and women. The attitude (not the legal case) that women should get what they deserve and therefore be forced into combat roles just like men is an immature male response born of bitterness, completely undermining a man's warrior responsibilities. First of all, not all women think they are equal to men. Many women are deeply appreciative of men for the sacrifices they make in war. So it is unfair to say, "Women deserve what they get." However, I understand how society functions and that the general mindset of our culture is deviant feminism. Regardless, we can't just throw our ethics or our purposes to the wind—otherwise, we're doomed as a civil society. The goal should not be exposing women to more danger because of the folly of feminism, but to change the ethos of culture and bring it back to a right understanding of men and women.

While the acrid feelings men have today regarding women in combat are understandable, I want to remind men of who they are. If you hope to make masculinity great again, you have to stop reacting to women in ways that reduce you as a man and put women in harm's way. The military issue is a prime example. Yes, feminists have been obnoxious and foolish regarding their notion of equal outcomes. They have been short-sighted about wanting "some" women to serve in combat, not realizing that, if the military makes it possible for a few women to serve in that capacity, then, legally, they have to require all women serve in that capacity with the possibility of a draft through selective service registration.

Unfortunately, many people who say, "If a woman can meet the qualifications, then she should be allowed to serve in combat," don't realize this has opened the door to lowering standards. Making it easier for a woman to succeed is an unintended consequence that often happens in these faux equality cases, and it has made the selective service exception clause for women null and void. Many women are shocked when they hear this, saying, "We didn't intend for that to happen. I don't want my daughter to be forced into war if the draft were ever reinstated."

The response of many men tired of feminist demands is, "Too damn bad. You asked for it, you got it. Equality. Our sons lose limbs, your daughters can lose them too. Our sons die, so will your daughters."

## Instead of exposing women to harm, men need to push back against the feminist narrative.

This situation is tragic and an example of how one wrong move is piled onto the next through mere reaction. The solution is to understand the purposes of men and women and the limitations of masculinity and femininity. No, women are not equal to men physically. Even the rare elite female with developed physical form cannot match her male elite counterpart. Most people are average and, among the average, men are physically stronger than women. The quest for equality of outcomes regarding physicality has been a disaster. Some cite Israel and the Kurds as examples of women successfully serving in combat, but these are very unusual situations in which these countries are small and surrounded by hostile enemies and in need of all hands on deck. This makes it a necessity; it doesn't make it right. Additionally, Israel Defense Forces don't put women in direct combat special operations, and they don't serve in the frontline brigades that face heavy warfare. They merely guard less hostile borders, where they are protected by men who face the harder battles.

When feminists aren't trying to milk the Israel situation for all that it's not, they sight fiction. "Look how powerful Arya Stark is!!" This is silly. We don't live in fantasy films with female heroines who magically fight just like the men. There aren't any Briennes of Tarth from *Game of Thrones* who can hold their own with elite male warriors of the same training. Wonder Woman is a fairytale. These fictional characters, however, seep into our cultural consciousness, seducing us into a living fiction that will ultimately get men and women killed. A woman has profound and powerful purposes in this life, but physically defending men isn't one of them. Even if she can do so through the help of technology, this calling isn't engrafted into her soul and her identity like it is a man's.

As for men and their response to this situation feminists have brought onto us, please remember a man's purpose and don't focus on feelings. No matter what a woman does or how she behaves, a man's responsibility as a man is to be a man. I know I'm treading very close to the dreaded "man-up" exhortation, but you won't ever be treated like a man if you abandon being a man. This doesn't mean you should be a doormat in your personal life—essential to being a man *is not* being a doormat, but a leader who brings order to chaos—and part of that order is respectfully reminding a woman that her purpose is not the same as yours.

Responding to feminized policies and social trends like this means that men should push back against feminist insanity and take up their position on the perimeter of society regarding bad policy or warfare. As author David Carter writes:

> A society that ignores and overrules the natural capacity and instinct of the male to protect hearth and home, and the unique strength and instinct of the female to bring new life and nurture the family, is a society that has signed its own death warrant. One of the reasons I spent twenty years in uniform, deploying to any number of the world's hell holes, was so I could face the monsters over there, rather than having my family face them over here. The concept of protecting what

> in gentler times was called "the fairer sex" wasn't antiquated at all, but rather an honor and a duty.[93]

This is what traditional masculinity looks like. Real men defend those they love, even when they're not appreciated because they see beyond themselves and even their current cultural climate. They see the future and want what's best for society. They see the God who made them and who has directed them to defend women, the elderly, and those who can't protect themselves, no matter the cost to their own bodies. They remain loyal to principle, truth, duty, and honor because this is objectively good and right. They don't get caught up in the subjective arguments of a culture awash in moral relativism. They hone their skills, clear their thinking, steel their hearts for the battle, and remember the love that drives them ever forward.

## WEAKLINGS AND ABUSERS DISRUPT THE WORKPLACE, FUELING HOSTILITY BETWEEN MEN AND WOMEN.

One of the more understated archetypes of masculinity is that of the sage or prophet, the wise man who has in-depth knowledge, insight, and intuition. They bring these qualities to their relationships and their service in the home, religious institutions, schools, and the workplace. A man's purpose as the sage is not only to work for his own self-interest, but to help others discover who they are, what skills they bring to the world, and how to succeed in all they do. They're the Obi-Wan Kenobis who teach how to master the Force for good. They are the Merlins who guide kings to create a better life for everyone. They're the Nathans who confront unfaithful Davids, so they'll admit their sin and seek repentance. They are the prophets who speak from the mountaintop, guiding the people in the direction they should go and warning them of threats and pitfalls.

Whenever I pick up a book that is instruction about life, I feel as if I'm in the presence of a master. C. S. Lewis taught me to be reconciled to the mysteries of God in *Till We Have Faces*, and he showed me the futility of subjectivism and moral relativism as I read about the floating islands of *Perelandra* and the heroine's desire to find the fixed island. He showed me the path of redemption as I read of Ransom's journey from the dark, watery depths of that island to its sunlit peaks, and I saw my own life, the loneliness of it, the frustrations, fears, and hopes that drive me upward.

When I read of the life of author Shelby Steele, I'm humbled by the message of a black man who experienced life before the Civil Rights movement yet refused to make others feel guilty for transgressions they did not commit. His honesty and insight challenge me to think differently about my own history and my present realities. The history books of Paul Johnson, the poems of Donne and Keats, the works of Shakespeare, and the ancient texts of philosophers, scholastics, and intellectuals—these and countless others are masters to us all, teaching us knowledge about ourselves and the life we share.

Masters of music, inventors of technology, and creators of art that use intuition and skill to build civilization—all of these are like magicians using their powers to create and transform their imaginations into reality. We see this most often in the workplace, where people labor together to order their particular world. Whatever it is, whatever you do, you are using knowledge to maintain society or propel it forward. When people engage in their craft and apply their knowledge for the betterment of the world, it is a beautiful thing to behold, just as it's repulsive when their motivation is selfish.

## Manipulators in the workplace damage relationships because they only care about themselves.

Immature men who fail to be the prophets they are designed to be can cause a lot of damage. Instead of using their insight and intuition for good, they seek their own glory and power. This transforms them into manipulators and tricksters who rob coworkers and employees of opportunities, the knowledge they need to succeed, or the fruits of their labors. They can do this individually or as part an immature "boys club." We've seen these at work in the worst way when sexual harassment and abuse happens in the workplace as men cover for one another. We've seen it in businesses where employers exploit employees by not paying them what they deserve or by working them like slaves. We've seen it when good workers are abandoned or undermined when they should be championed. Instead of doing what is right, immature men only promote what benefits them.

While working on this book, I was fired from two media outlets for a tweet I wrote in response to a gay journalist whom I saw as egging on hundreds of people who were attacking my husband and accusing him of abusing me simply because he made a joke that I should keep quiet while he watched the end of a close basketball game. Because I'm an anti-feminist, my husband and I have running "sexist" jokes in the house. They mean nothing and are hardly representative of reality. My husband is kind, giving, and loving, and he didn't deserve to be falsely accused of a crime. I take full responsibility for the consequences of being a provocative writer, but I had attacked no one. I was sharing an inside joke. Countless people responding to it with threats, false accusations, and smears against a private citizen wasn't acceptable.

After I tweeted my angry response, I was fired. It was a heartbreaking end to years of building a platform in journalism and working hard to develop my career after staying at home to raise six children. The men who "cut off our association" both knew me and had published enough of my writings to know I'm not a bigot. One was even a good friend who had known me for years. While I disagree with the moral foundation of LGBT, I respect homosexual rights and freedoms and see them as fellow human beings who deserve love and compassion. I failed at that because I was rightly angry, but I'm no bigot. Journalist Eddie Scarry at the *Washington Examiner* agreed:

> No one who has suffered through the insufferable Twitter mob can blame her for her temporary insanity. It is hell to sit through what McAllister undoubtedly knew would be days' worth of nameless, pictureless people in her Twitter mentions, attempting to shame her for expressing a view that isn't uncommon—which can essentially be summed up as "pick and choose your marital battles." McAllister hit back at [the journalist] where she thought it might hurt because she knew what he was encouraging the Twitter mob to do to her. That doesn't automatically make her a homophobe. It makes her a righteously angry woman.[94]

Regardless, according to my publishers, I had to go—the threat of being associated with a so-called "homophobe" who had been labeled as such by leftists in the media couldn't be tolerated, much less defended.

I apologized for the harshness of the tweet, and I explained to both my employers that I was protecting my husband—albeit badly—who had been attacked, and I had lashed out in his defense. It didn't matter. Even though both outlets defended free speech on social media and one had assured its writers that they would never be fired for anything they said on Twitter, they let me go. And, by doing so, they reinforced the lie that I was homophobic, a label that is slapped on conservatives by leftists to silence and delegitimize them.

Many people came to my defense because they understood what had happened. But it didn't change my circumstances. Ironically, not long after I had been let go from these outlets, one of the publishers became angry when his wife, who is a public figure, got into a scrap on a late-night talk show. In response to the show's host, my former boss tweeted a rant that was just as "homophobic" as mine. The media exploded in criticism of him, of course. But he wasn't let go from his position at the publication that fired me. On the contrary, when he apologized and insisted that he was merely defending his wife, he was praised by the very same people who had lashed out at me, attacked me, and even threatened me. People in the conservative media who applauded my firing rallied around him. Others saw the hypocrisy and wondered what was going on. Why did men who had dumped on me support another man who had done the same thing? Was it about sex differences, or was it about power since he was in a higher professional position than I was? It didn't matter if it was about my sex or the jobs we held, because the root problem was immature men failing to be the men they're called to be in the workplace. They put self-interest and alliances that benefitted them above fairness and loyalty to someone who had been falsely accused.

A man who works in political media told me after this happened that it was the boys club in action. Men are sometimes going to surround other men who are attacked, especially if they are integral to a power dynamic. They'll sacrifice anyone else to the wolves. These men were merely looking out for number one, to protect their alliances and their brands. They were certainly free to do that, but business interests don't stop people from being morally accountable when they walk through the doors of their profession.

My business—the media—is full of immature men who keep others from succeeding when they should be supporting them, who use others as stepping-stones to their own success, and who abuse women because they have an inflated sense of self and think only in terms of power dynamics. Many industries are like this. If you are a man who is making decisions only for yourself, no matter what happens to others, you're not a masculine man. You're a manipulator. If you lie to your employees or coworkers, if you promise them advancements or opportunities with no intention to deliver, if you're a boss and you fail to develop your employees to their greatest potential, and if you fail to use the insight you have into others' abilities and personalities for the good, then you are no real man. You are a pretender.

## Men who denigrate the successes of others are immature men weakened by insecurity.

Some men in the workplace don't just fail to use their knowledge and authority for the benefit of others; they use their insight to sabotage those who succeed. They're snakes in the office. They're lazy. They cut corners. And they constantly put down others who have more achievements than them. I used to work as an advertising salesperson for a newspaper, and there was a man there who had several established accounts. Instead of working hard to develop more clients, he skated by on the ones he had. He would go to long lunches instead of going out on sales calls. When he'd arrive back in the office, he'd walk around and point out things other salespeople were doing wrong. "That ad won't attract the buyers you want." "Still trying to get that car dealership to sign on? Never going to happen!" One of the worst things he said to me was, "The only reason you got that sale was Gerald down at the furniture store was looking at your legs." Not cool. And not a real man.

The lazy mentality of the failed prophet is rampant in our society. How often do we see the successful disparaged? The false notion of "white privilege" is one manifestation of the impotent prophet. "Other people have more, so they must be privileged." It couldn't possibly be that they have more profitable talents and abilities, that they've worked harder, or that they are part of a family that has strived to succeed and the children benefit from those earnings. Instead, we too often see those who have succeeded pulled down instead of those who have failed pulled up. This is why attacks on masculinity are particularly dangerous. Masculinity honors others instead of coveting what they have. It infuses culture with self-knowledge, a desire to be better, know more, and be the best. Masculinity looks deep into the soul and waters the seeds that have been planted by God. It sees people as possibilities in their own right, inspired by their hopes and dreams.

Instead, we have a society that imposes the will and ideologies of the powerful onto others. You are labeled according to the dictates of a politically correct culture. You are robbed of true knowledge and taught propaganda instead of truth. You are diminished by those who covet what you have accomplished. You are told lies are truth, bitter is sweet, and evil is good. Knowledge is suppressed or twisted according to the subjective will of the powerful. Those in authority are not the most numerous. Often, they're merely the loudest, the most sympathetic, and those that engender guilt in others to compel them to pay reparations for things they never did.

## HEALING COMES THROUGH RESTORING KNOWLEDGE OF OUR TRUE IDENTITIES AND LOVING EACH OTHER FOR WHO WE ARE.

A fundamental toxicity in our society isn't toxic masculinity. It is men and women not living according to their design and purpose. It's people not knowing who they truly are. The only way our society, families, and institutions can truly be free to pursue happiness is to revive our humanity in the image of God and live the meaningful, responsible lives we were meant to live—with acts of love.

Men are their best when they are living as God intended, according to the dictates of love and in relationship with others. Anything else leads to suffering and despair. Sometimes that pain is just below the surface. It's covered in layers of distractions, but it's real. They feel it in their hearts, and it radiates outward onto others they're meant to love but can't or won't. Most want to be free of the despair, the loneliness that shrouds them, and women can help them instead of digging the dagger deeper into their hearts. Women can bring the positive changes they want, not by reconstructing masculinity but by appreciating it. They need to listen to the men in their lives, and the most important thing they're saying is, "Respect me as a man, walk with me as we journey through this world together, know me as I am, and simply love me."

CHAPTER 9

# CRISIS OF IDENTITY

*Men go abroad to admire the heights of mountains, the mighty waves of the sea, the broad tides of rivers, the compass of the ocean, and the circuits of the stars, yet pass over the mystery of themselves without a thought.*

—Augustine

"I just don't know who I'm supposed to be," my friend said. Now in his early fifties, he had changed careers, his children were grown, and his relationship with his wife was rocky at best. He didn't say, but I suspected sex had become nonexistent. I listened as he poured out his frustrations about growing up with a distant dad, dealing with a self-absorbed mother, and mourning the loss of a promising career. "I just want to disappear," he said. As I listened to him, I felt like he already had. He was lost, his pain revealing much more than the struggles of a career change. He was looking into a mirror and not recognizing the person he saw.

Who was he—A father? A husband? An engineer? A Christian? What defined him, and why did he feel so unsettled? The wounds many men have because of father issues were evident as we talked, and I knew that, as a woman, I couldn't help him traverse this path. He needed a man to validate his masculinity and find the missing pieces his father left scattered throughout his childhood. He was a man drifting on detached, floating islands, desperately swimming from one to the other but finding no solid ground. He was focusing on his circumstances, his abilities, how others treated him, and the roles he filled. He was fixated on what he didn't have, what he had lost, and what he "should" be. His feelings about himself and others were defining his nature and purpose. The ethos of our anti-male culture only added to his angst.

I've seen this struggle countless times—people desperately trying to figure out their place in this world and discover who they're meant to be. They flounder in their frustrations, expectations, and fears. I wanted to reach out and hold my friend—a very feminine response. I wanted to soothe away his pain and push back the isolating effects of an unappreciative society. I wanted to help him find himself, so he could be free. But I knew he—like so many others—needed more than a hug and words of comfort. He needed something solid to stand on. He needed a mountain in the midst of a turbulent sea.

We've all been there at some point: riddled with anxieties, struggles, and loneliness. We're like Jacob wrestling with God through the dark night until we stop fighting and see him face-to-face in the morning light. In seeing God, we finally see ourselves for who we are. The struggle is frightening and depressing. We feel alone. We feel abandoned. We feel adrift. When we let feelings rule us, we experience a kind of inner chaos that leaves us anxious and unsettled. To find order and peace, we need to assert our minds over our emotions. We need to bring our core principles to the fore and let them guide our lives like reins steering a powerful beast. This is as true for whole communities as it is for individuals. America is facing a crisis of identity, and we're allowing feelings and fear-laden ideologies define who we are. The result has been chaos. We're spiraling downward, and it's time to stop and get reordered.

One of the most insidious and debilitating problems we're facing in America today has to do with this issue of identity. What does it mean to be human? What does it mean to be male or female? Can we learn from each other to discover the answers? Do we share common threads? These questions plague us, and very few are looking for a solution because they don't realize the nature of the problem. In this chapter, I aim to address that problem. This discussion is heavy on the philosophical, but it's necessary. It's meat for those who are starving. It's the cornerstone of the building we wish to construct. If we don't have our foundations right, everything else will crumble.

## IDENTITY INCLUDES THREE FACETS: HUMANITY, SEXUALITY, AND INDIVIDUALITY.

To begin, I want you to picture an umbrella in your mind. Our identity is that umbrella with our humanity at the top as the canopy. Our sexuality is the shaft that descends into the handle. And, finally, our individuality is the rib structure beneath the canopy. The canopy is broad and includes commonality with everyone. Our humanity is the most objective attribute to our identity. In this, we are all the same. No one on earth, as far as we know, is an alien with DNA from another planet. We're human. In our shared humanity, we are connected to and just like everyone else—as we look into the faces of people from all over the world, no matter their size, color, race, or sex, we see a reflection of ourselves as human beings.

Beneath the canopy is the shaft that extends into the handle where our shared identity as human beings begins to diverge. Men and women are not the same, but each group shares universal, objective traits. To one degree or another, all men embody the same masculine characteristics, and all women share the same feminine attributes. Our bodies alone are a testament to this fact, though there are innate qualities we also share. If our identity stopped there, however, we wouldn't see much diversity in life—just two sexual groupings with no distinctiveness beyond masculinity and femininity. To see people only according to their sexuality is to impose a limited identity onto them. The umbrella won't open into all of its glory.

Too many religious sects and secular ideologies fall into this trap. They force all men into the same identity without any individual distinctiveness, and they treat women the same (often more so than men). We see manifestations of this in identity politics. Some of the worst offenders today are feminists who have made their ideology of female empowerment a religion of its own. They force all women into the same mold, expecting them to share the same personal goals, march in the same parades, and vote for the same candidates. Any ideology that reduces people to a single aspect of their identity fails to see them as fully integrated human beings with shared as well as wholly personal attributes.

Clearly, our sexuality isn't the sum of our identity. We are unique individuals—the ribs that spread out beneath the canopy from the shaft. We are both united with others in our humanity and our shared sexuality, but we are also distinct. This distinction can't be the entirety of our identity, but neither can it be ignored as if we're just the same as everyone else. We are the whole umbrella—human, male or female, and an individual. A canopy without the rest is not an umbrella. The same is true with the shaft or the ribs. The umbrella—your identity—is made up of three inseparable parts.

**Our identity as human beings is to be made in the image of God.**

Too many of us try to discover ourselves without a stable worldview to help answer the question, "Who am I?" The most basic answer is that we are made in the image of God—unique among all creatures. Being human is being the image-bearer of the divine and is the foundation of everything we are and might become. This is an identity every human being who has ever existed shares. We aren't mere mortals or simple materialistic forms, but spiritual beings designed as caretakers of the world, to create, overcome evil, shine the light of glory in darkness, and, most of all, to love—not a squishy, romantic, Hollywood-crafted love—but real *agape* love with its emphasis on giving rather than taking.

We often don't consider love when we think of our identity, but it is the core of our nature. It is a state of being as much as an action. God is love, and if we are made in his image, we are love. God made us out of his own love—to love and to be loved. Everything about us stems from this reality and should define us as men, as women, and as individuals. "Love," I told my friend as he wrestled with finding himself. "Start there. That's who you are at your core, and everything else is a manifestation of that, a reflection of God in the world and in other people."

If only we saw ourselves in this way—if we started our journey of self-discovery here—we would live very different lives. But it is the one thing we most often seem to forget, mainly because love has been so overused and watered down by our silly, shallow, sexualized, self-indulgent culture. We reduce it to romanticism, failing to see our humanity as the very manifestation of love. *Eros* rules over all other loves like a seductive tyrant from *Brave New World*. Self-love hides the face of God. We cover his image with labels, professions, materialism, doctrines, delusions, dogma, and pathologies. We project our ideas about ourselves onto others, searching for our self-made image in their faces and becoming angry when we don't see it. Instead of seeing others for who they are—images of God's love—we see a blank space that we arrogantly assume is our right to color. We use other people as a means to further our quest for identity instead of loving them as they are.

Love is certainly a missing piece in the relationship between men and women today. The ancient war of the sexes is ongoing, and we see it in the modern feminist movement's hostility toward men. Pride, vengeance, and power drive much of feminism today, and only a revival of substantial love will heal the damage feminism has wrought. Only love—and the trust that undergirds it—will rebuild the broken relationships between men and women. Everything we discuss in this book drives to that ultimate solution. It is the foundation for every relationship. It alone is the healing salve that can cure the wounds inflicted by selfish ideologies.

Unfortunately, we hear a lot more about personal liberty instead of love. Doing what we want takes priority over doing for others. We separate two qualities that should always go together: love and liberty. Love is intrinsically connected to freedom, and freedom is essential to our identity as human beings. God endowed us with free will. We are not designed to live under the oppressive control of other human beings or even of God. This freedom from God is not autonomy in the true sense of the word. We are all under his sovereignty and made by his hand. He is ultimately in control of all he created, but he has chosen to let us be free to act. While our choices, thoughts, and movements through this world are free of his direct control, our nature as created is not. God made man in his image, and key to that image is the freedom to make choices without the imposition of another's will. We can choose to eat from the tree of the knowledge of good and evil or not. We can choose to love or to hate. We wouldn't be human without free will, and we wouldn't be made in God's image if we were mere automatons.

This freedom is a great gift and a profound responsibility. In making human beings free, God created the possibility that they would choose to do wrong, to be hateful instead of loving, or to proudly exalt themselves to greater heights over their created order rather than live humbly and freely within it. A free humanity was worth the risk because the key to being human is exercising the greatest free act of all and the singular purpose of human existence: to love. We cannot love if we aren't free to choose to love, but being free to love means we might choose to hate. We certainly see the latter in the feminist war against men today—a war that has led to a twisted understanding of what it means to be male and female, even to the point of erasing differences in the quest for independence.

## When God made humanity, he made them male and female.

In his *Space Trilogy*, C. S. Lewis gives a stunning portrait of masculinity and femininity when he describes two creatures from different worlds. He focuses not on their physical "sex," but on the essence of their distinct sexuality as part of the image of God. The creature from Malacandra is masculine, and the one from Perelandra is female: Malacandra has "the look of one standing armed, at the ramparts of his own remote archaic world, in ceaseless vigilance, his eyes ever roaming the earthward horizon whence his danger came long ago." Those eyes have the sailor's look, Lewis writes, "Eyes that are impregnated with distance." The eyes of the feminine, Perelandra, "opened, as it were, inward, as if they were the curtained gateway to a world of waves and murmurings and wandering airs, of life that rocked in winds and splashed on mossy stones and descended as the dew and arose sunward in thin-spun delicacy of mist." Malacandra is made of stone and, in Perelandra, the lands swim across the water. "My eyes," the narrator says, "have seen Mars and Venus. I have seen Ares and Aphrodite."[95]

The distinctiveness of the masculine and feminine as they're reflected in the male and female is losing ground today. Femininity is on the rise like a flood beating against the hard rock of masculinity, crushing it to pieces, beating it down until it is soft and smooth. Men, who are designed to be strong, are made to feel useless in a world in which their masculinity has been devalued, denigrated, and hated. The two most significant distinctive aspects of human identity that create the foundational relationship of human existence and freedom are at war with each other when they should be at peace.

There have been long periods in human history when men had the upper hand, draining women of their vibrancy, burning them to vapor instead of diving into their depths. The result was hardness, a cruel and unbending quality that robbed life of the fluid power of femininity. Feminism was initially a reaction to this masculine dominance. But now the roles are reversed, and women are the aggressors, drowning life instead of giving it.

As humans, we are created as two separate but socially connected beings designed to love each other—male and female, the rock and the water. Both are facets of the image of God, which—when they come together as one—reveal the human completion of that image. Because God is spirit, our masculine and feminine sexuality is more than just our physical form, though the material form is a manifestation of spiritual realities. This spiritual context of masculinity and femininity was once understood as "gender," but now this word has been distorted to mean basically the same as "sex." Masculinity now means whatever someone wants it to mean. The same is true with femininity. These two essences have been severed from their physical manifestations, allowing for (in the deluded mind) the female to be predominantly masculine and the male to be predominantly feminine. This perversion of sexuality is contrary to God's design and reality. While masculinity doesn't equal male and femininity doesn't equal female, male is a reflection of masculinity and female is a reflection of femininity. Our spiritual and physical human identity, which incorporates our sexuality, is cohesive. It can't be cut apart to make a new cloth without destroying humanity itself.

God universally designed masculinity in a way that is fixed in his divine identity. Our individual preferences, feelings, cultural proclivities, and particularities—good or bad—don't change that identity. To be male is to be made in the image of God as part of our humanity. The same is true of the female. The divine feminine and masculine essences are mixed into both males and females, but the male is mostly masculine, and the female is primarily feminine. Her physical makeup reflects this fact (even for the most "masculine" women), including her brain function and her body. The same is true for men. To twist this, to change it, to use technology to distort nature as God designed it is to impose an emotional or psychological pathology onto it. This sexuality confusion corrupts God's design and deviates from his purposes for men and women. It opens the floodgates of chaos where there should be order. Ultimately, it isolates us because we are made to relate to one another as males and females, not as social reconstructions. We cannot rightly love one another in the midst of confusion. In that space, we can only survive, react, and vie for power.

We hear a lot about sexuality being socially constructed. The expression of it certainly is in countless ways, but the core reality of it is not, no more than our humanity is socially constructed. Have you ever heard a reasonable person say that our humanity is socially constructed? Of course not—because that would be nonsensical, though that is the direction our society is headed. The same is true with our sexuality. We would have to be blind to think otherwise, and I'm afraid we're becoming a blind society.

To be "socially constructed" according to our nature is to be manipulated by other human beings. This is a frightening thought, and it puts us in the hands of others to be controlled, even as we imagine we are controlling ourselves. The only safeguard to the tyranny of social construction is to understand that we are divinely constructed by an objective reality that can't be changed but only twisted or manipulated by human beings. Our sexuality is not defined by humans—not by the state, psychologists, religious institutions, a deviant culture, and not even ourselves. It is defined by God. A man is made to protect, provide, and lead his family in love and goodness as a reflection of God's holiness in this world. A woman is made to create life, nurture it, influence her husband as a queen ruling at his side, and complement him in love and as an image-bearer of God's glory. Our sexuality is rooted in a solid foundation that makes us human. Any subversion of it is inherently dehumanizing and destructive.

America is a nation built on the core principle that our rights do not come from men, but from God. Our rights come from God because *we* come from God. Our identity does not come from men any more than our rights do, and the same oppression is waiting for us if we think otherwise. This man-centered and materialistic notion is the core cause of America's identity crisis. We are in the process of rejecting the objective foundation of humanity itself. We are caught in the matrix of a wicked ideology which asserts that not only are our rights determined by man, but our very nature is. If we don't stop this trajectory, we won't only lose our liberty; we will lose ourselves.

## Our individual identity is shared by no one else.

Being divinely constructed does not mean predetermined realities control us. It doesn't mean human religious institutions dictate how we live. It doesn't mean we are all the same, living in a religious Borg collective. There is more to our identity than shared humanity and sexuality. We are each unique individuals and we have free will—not to be something we're not, but to express ourselves in varied ways as we live out our purposes in society. The beauty, creativity, and complexity of the God who made the universe in all its diversity are revealed through individuality. While I share a common humanity with you and all the morality that entails, and, if you're a woman, I share common traits as a female, I am still an individual with looks, qualities, talents, experiences, histories, struggles, and perspectives that are all my own. These don't contradict my humanity or my sexuality, but they are mine. My life might not look like yours, and it shouldn't. My distinctiveness enhances the world as I infuse my personal identity into the human community, and the same is true of you.

When we think of identity, we usually think of the individual distinctiveness first and, mistakenly, let this limited identity determine everything about us. We make the individual the canopy, with our desires, feelings, abilities, and beliefs redefining what it means to be a man or woman and even, in its most twisted manifestation, what it means to be human. I call this the tyranny of the subjective. But there is another kind of tyranny—the kind that refuses to allow the individual to be the unique person he or she is. The horror of totalitarianism, whether secular or religious, is that it reduces all people to a common denominator as defined by the powerful. Tyranny of an individual or a collective group is contrary to God's design because he made each of us special. Only when we respect other individuals will we truly appreciate and love one another as image-bearers of the One who made the stars in the sky, planets that fill the universe, birds of the air, insects in the woods and fields, fish in the sea, and every grain of sand on the shore. The diversity of existence is breathtaking. To snuff out individuality or try to reduce it is an abomination and an attack on the God who makes all things beautiful. It is the opposite of love.

## WE NEED TO KNOW WHO WE ARE BEFORE WE CAN UNDERSTAND EACH OTHER.

Identity—"who we are" might seem like a simple thing, but we are witnessing that it is not, particularly when we refuse to look to the roadmap that has been provided for us. Instead, we believe identity is determined by our feelings and instincts, to be reinvented at will. We *define* ourselves instead of *discovering* ourselves. The former assumes ontological autonomy, as if we created ourselves, while the latter rightly assumes a reality that is objectively established. Objectivity brings order and virtue, whereas subjectivity alone creates chaos. Likewise, objectivity alone erases distinctiveness. We need both—with objectivity as the foundation, not vice versa. "I cannot merely make myself over in the image constructed by my intellect (particularly if that intellect is possessed by an ideology)," Jordan Peterson writes in *12 Rules for Life*. "I have a nature, and so do you, and so do we all. We must discover that nature, and contend with it, before making peace with ourselves. What is it that we most truly are? What is it that we could most truly become, knowing who we most truly are? We must get to the very bottom of things before such questions can be truly answered."[96]

We all come to a point in life when we ask ourselves what we want to do and *who* we want to be. Good parents train their children to help them get to know themselves and develop that knowledge as productive, loving, virtuous members of society. Admittedly, part of that training is parents "imposing" an identity onto children to help them live within a specific culture, and parents, not strangers, are tasked with this essential responsibility. We are social creatures, after all, and need to fit within the context of society. Mature fathers are particularly adept at this task. They have the insight and knowledge of being human, of a boy becoming a man and a girl becoming a woman. They lead the child into knowledge of himself and how he fits into the family and society.

This training, however, doesn't mean the child's human nature or his sexuality is reconstructed and redefined according to another's will—an individual parent or a social group. It should be an elegant convergence of self-knowledge and influential knowledge of others as a child matures. A child left to himself to determine his reality and nature based on his immature ideas or feelings is a disservice to the child, if not abusive. Just as bad is an adult imposing his will for the sake of reconstructing the child into an image that reflects the adult and not the child as God fashioned him. To grow in self-knowledge and a proper understanding of identity requires a foundation that is beyond the child and anyone else. That reality is expressed as natural law, the way of God, and the design of creation. To make it anything else is subjective tyranny.

Our society is currently losing touch with this foundation of identity. We don't understand who we are or our purpose as human beings, and we certainly don't know what it means to be male or female. We're so lost that we imagine a hundred different sexes or "genders." Feminists have distorted equality with men into sameness under the guise of equality. In our modern quest to conquer nature and bring it under subjection through technology, pathological notions, and secular ideologies, we seek to transform human nature itself. We strive to cut it out from a new cloth and reshape it any way we desire. That which is traditional has been tossed into the postmodern abyss. "Men have sacrificed their own share in traditional humanity to devote themselves to the task of deciding what 'Humanity' shall henceforth mean," C. S. Lewis writes in *Abolition of Man*.[97] Instead of discovering the pattern of humanity and sexuality handed to us, created within us, we are making new blueprints for ourselves—and, if we can make blueprints, then other people can make them for us. "For the power of Man to make himself what he pleases means, as we have seen, the power of some men to make other men what they please,"[98] Lewis wisely observed.

Teachers and parents once initiated the young into established knowledge about sexuality, but now anything goes. Feelings and political agendas dictate reality, not the other way around—often in the name of freedom. We once experienced liberty within the frame of objective values and truths, but that is quickly being abandoned today—to our detriment. Subjectivity has been unleashed across the American landscape, and it is devouring everything in sight like a wild animal. In the past, teachers "did not cut men to some pattern they had chosen," Lewis writes. "They handed on what they had received: they initiated the young neophyte into the mystery of humanity which over-arched him and them alike. It was but old birds teaching young birds to fly."[99] This commitment to objective values is no longer the case. We now posit truth and human nature as subjective constructs and misinterpret freedom as cutting away from reality instead of living within it.

## Feelings don't determine reality or identity.

The irony of America's understanding of identity today is that we are heading toward totalitarianism in the name of individuality. In this new postmodern world, the individual—the most subjective aspect of our identity—dictates our humanity and sexuality. For example, if the individual thinks it's her right to demand another person give her his earnings because she believes she deserves it, she is allowing her desires—no matter how economically justified—to overrule another person's right to their property. If a woman feels like she's a man and can do *anything* a man can do, particularly ignoring his greater physical strength, she pushes the man out of the way or changes the rules to legitimize her fantasy. Her desire to do what a man does and be as a man overrules her objective nature as a female and degrades the man as a distinctive male.

Whatever we do, whatever we want to be, however we want to express ourselves, we need to ask ourselves:

1. Is it loving, and is it right according to God?
2. Is it true to my purpose as a human?
3. If I'm a woman, is it true to my purpose as a female? If I'm a man, is it true to my purpose as a male?
4. Is it true to my purpose as an individual?

We need to answer these questions and be able to say yes to each if we want order in our lives. The umbrella of our identity must be opened in all its fullness without contradiction. This self-discovery in light of objective reality is how we achieve balance of unity and diversity in society.

When we ignore the full breadth of identity from the universals of being human, to the objective nature of sexuality, to the unique qualities of the individual, we let the shifting preferences of people—not God—become the standard for everyone. An individual's tastes regarding hair color, dress, artistic expressions, or employment (especially for women) become the standard for all, with the tyrannical individual even claiming the manmade construct is objective and designed by God. On this faulty basis, he dictates to others what they can and cannot do when nothing about having pink hair, going to work with kids at home, or being a rock musician violates God's objective design for human beings or a particular sex. If you're thinking of the old movie *Footloose*, when the kids weren't allowed to dance, it fits. The will of the individual (in that case, the preacher) becomes the dominant "objective" reality for all human beings, and that individual uses his power to recreate reality and legitimize a fantasy.

I've seen this despotic individuality in politics as personal feelings dictate policy and even morality—sometimes to the point of intruding on another person's freedom and rights. The girl who wants to be referred to with the pronoun "he" makes her personal desires a universal reality binding everyone else to comply with her wishes instead of her sexual reality. Professionals lose their jobs if they don't conform, people are kicked off of social media platforms, and sometimes lives are even threatened. All because someone has exalted their individual preferences and pathologies into the objective realm of humanity, demanding compliance under the threat of punishment.

Historically, we've seen the tyranny of subjectivism in totalitarian regimes that impose the state's will onto individuals to the point of executing them in gas chambers if they don't comply. Truth, facts, and human nature itself are twisted into whatever those in power want it to be. The individual—the Borg Queen—forces everyone else into the collective to bow to her subjective truth, to assimilate her lies. She is the only "I" among the "We." And so, the individual who has defied objective value becomes the enemy of individuality. "Before mass leaders seize the power to fit reality to their lies, the propaganda is marked by its extreme contempt for facts as such, for in their opinion fact depends entirely on the power of the man who can fabricate it," Hannah Ardent writes in *The Origins of Totalitarianism*. "The outstanding negative quality of the totalitarian elite is that it never stops to think about the world as it really is [or people as they truly are] and never compares the lies with reality."[100]

## Our identities are cohesive, not cutouts pasted into something new.

We run into serious problems when we allow our good and natural desires, abilities, and inclinations to dictate what it means to be human or male and female. We create atrocities when we allow our pathologies, dysfunctions, disorders, and sins to determine our identity. A man, for example, who believes that women are servants or sexual objects to cater only to his will is not seeing each woman as first, a human being with innate rights; second, as a woman who is not a sexual pawn to be used by others but to be cherished and loved; or third, as an individual with her unique qualities that are unlike his.

Getting to know ourselves in light of God's image in us and then getting to know others is one of the great necessities and adventures of life. When we corrupt or twist it, we are robbing ourselves of a fully integrated and peaceful existence. We are making ourselves the center of the universe, the determiner of truth, identity, and reality. We are making ourselves God. When we establish ourselves as the center, our subjectivity the truth, then we stand alone with no common threads holding us to other people. When we are alone, we cannot love. When we cannot love, we seek cruel ways to force other people to join us in our circle of one. This deep loneliness and its resultant oppression are diseases infecting America today.

Human identity is complex, fully integrated, and objectively designed while subjectively expressed. It is inherently social with the primary purpose of loving others through *agape*, *philia*, and *erotic* love. Misalignments in any aspect of our humanity, failure to see the commonalities we have with other humans in our general design, as well as our particular sexuality, is a disruption to self-knowledge and our understanding of other people. By rejecting the objective basis of our identity as humans, men and women, and even as individuals, we have become subjective islands unto ourselves vying for power instead of connecting through love. Hyperindividuality that puts human autonomy above God's sovereignty has reduced us to our feelings, fantasies, and fetishes. We declare that "we can be whatever we want to be," failing to see that, when making such a declaration, we have cut ourselves off from any connection with others, and we have exposed ourselves to being defined by those in power. Instead of seeing ourselves as fully integrated human beings with objective purposes and designs, we are ripping ourselves into pieces. We are shaping sexuality according to our desires and even our pathologies instead of seeing that our individuality is defined by our objectively designed sexuality, just as our humanity cannot be separated from who we are as individuals.

Masculinity, like femininity, is part of the matrix of humanity that cannot be recast by the individual. We can't take shears to ourselves in the name of autonomy without cutting ourselves to pieces, leaving us to be glued back together by someone with an agenda to make us into their image. The only image we reflect is the one created by God. We only know ourselves when we know him in Christ, when we set pride aside and humbly see ourselves through his eyes. When we look into his face, we see our own and we see others as they truly are—precious souls made in love, to love, and to be loved.

# ENDNOTES

1. Thomas Sowell, *Black Rednecks & White Liberals: Hope, Mercy, Justice and Autonomy in the American Health Care System* (New York: Encounter Books, 2009), Kindle.
2. C. S. Lewis, *Reflections on the Psalms* (New York: HarperOne, 2017), Kindle, 1–2.
3. Sowell, *Black Rednecks & White Liberals.*
4. Cortney O'Brien, "Having Taken Hit After 'Toxic Masculinity' Ad, Gillette Is Trying a New Campaign," Townhall, Townhall.com, August 22, 2019, https://townhall.com/tipsheet/cortneyobrien/2019/08/22/having-lost-millions-with-toxic-masculinity-ad-gillette-is-trying-a-new-campaign-n2552068.
5. Alexis de Tocqueville, *Democracy in America*—Volume 2 (1859), iBooks, https://books.apple.com/us/book/democracy-in-america-volume-2/id498732991.
6. Ibid.
7. John Crowther, ed., "No Fear Taming of the Shrew," Sparknotes LLC, 2004, https://www.sparknotes.com/nofear/shakespeare/shrew/page_246/.
8. Robert Moore and Douglas Gillette, *King, Warrior, Magician, Lover: Rediscovering the Archetypes of the Mature Masculine* (New York: HarperCollins, 1991), 7.
9. Ibid., xviii.

10 Chuck DeVore, "Fatal Employment: Men 10 Times More Likely Than Women to Be Killed at Work," *Forbes*, December 19, 2018, www.forbes.com/sites/chuckdevore/2018/12/19/fatal-employment-men-10-times-more-likely-than-women-to-be-killed-at-work/#33df277152e8.

11 Michael Kimmel, *Manhood in America: A Cultural History* (New York: The Free Press, a division of Simon and Schuster, 1996), 334–335.

12 Harper Lee, *To Kill a Mockingbird* (New York: HarperCollins, 2002).

13 Ibid.

14 Ibid.

15 Greg Hampikian, "Men, Who Needs Them?" *The New York Times*, August 24, 2012, www.nytimes.com/2012/08/25/opinion/men-who-needs-them.html.

16 Ibid.

17 Chris Field, "Man Down: The Attack on American Masculinity," *The Blaze*, December 13, 2018, www.theblaze.com/news/2014/11/04/man-down-the-attack-on-american-masculinity.

18 Michiko Kakutani, "Examining Women's Studies Programs," *The New York Times*, December 9, 1994, www.nytimes.com/1994/12/09/books/books-of-the-times-examining-women-s-studies-programs.html.

19 Alan M. Dershowitz, "The Bigotry of 'Intersectionality,'" *Gatestone Institute*, March 29, 2017, www.gatestoneinstitute.org/10131/the-bigotry-of-intersectionality.

20 "An Interview with Christina Hoff Sommers," *The Dartmouth Review*, February 27, 2017, dartreview.com/an-interview-with-christina-hoff-sommers/.

21 Ibid.

22 Christina Villegas, "The Modern Feminist Rejection of Constitutional Government," The Heritage Foundation, www.heritage.org/progressivism/report/the-modern-feminist-rejection-constitutional-government.

23 American Psychological Association, Boys and Men Guidelines Group. (2018). APA guidelines for psychological practice with boys and men. Retrieved from http://www.apa.org/about/policy/psychological-practice-boys-men-guidelines.pdf.

24 Ronald F. Levant and Gini Kopecky, *Masculinity Reconstructed: Changing the Rules of Manhood—At Work, in Relationships, and in Family Life* (New York: Plume/Penguin Books, 1996), 23.

25 Jocelyn Noveck, "Moms Killing Kids Not Nearly as Rare as We Think," NBCNews.com, NBCUniversal News Group, April 17, 2011, http://www.nbcnews.com/id/42634832/ns/us_news-crime_and_courts/t/moms-killing-kids-not-nearly-rare-we-think/#.XW61opNKip8.

26 "MGTOW," *MGTOW*, www.mgtow.com/.

27 Ibid.

28 Ibid.

29 Ibid.

30 Samantha Brick, "Catfights over Handbags and Tears in the Toilets. With Her Women-Only TV Company This Producer Thought She'd Kissed Goodbye to Conflict…" *Daily Mail Online*, Associated Newspapers, April 7, 2009, www.dailymail.co.uk/femail/article-1168182/Catfights-handbags-tears-toilets-When-producer-launched-women-TV-company-thought-shed-kissed-goodbye-conflict-.html.

31 Ibid.

32 Ibid.

33 Ibid.

[34] Villegas, "The Modern Feminist Rejection."
[35] Ibid.
[36] Brick, "Catfights over Handbags."
[37] *NCIS*, "Seadog," Season 1 Episode 3. Directed by Bradford May. Written by Donald P. Bellisario, Don McGill, and John C. Kelley (Belisarius Productions, Paramount Television, October 7, 2003).
[38] Moore and Gillette, *King, Warrior, Magician, Lover*, 98.
[39] Ibid.
[40] Ibid., 61–62.
[41] Judith S. Wallerstein and Joan B. Kelly, *Surviving the Breakup: How Children and Parents Cope with Divorce* (New York: BasicBooks, 2000).
[42] National Fatherhood Initiative, "The Father Absence Crisis in America," 2017, https://cdn2.hubspot.net/hub/135704/file-396018955-pdf/RyanNFIFatherAbsenceInfoGraphic051614.pdf.
[43] Gretchen Livingston et al., "8 Facts about American Dads," Pew Research Center, June 12, 2019, www.pewresearch.org/fact-tank/2018/06/13/fathers-day-facts/.
[44] Fathers for Life, "Children of Divorce & Separation—Statistics," April 11, 2001, fathersforlife.org/divorce/chldrndiv.htm.
[45] Sanford H. Braver et al., "Frequency of Visitation by Divorced Fathers: Differences in Reports by Fathers and Mothers," *American Journal of Orthopsychiatry* 61, no. 3 (1991): 448–454, http://dx.doi.org/10.1037/h0079260.
[46] Livingston et al., "8 Facts."
[47] Kim Parker et al., "On Gender Differences, No Consensus on Nature vs. Nurture," Pew Research Center's Social & Demographic Trends Project, January

22, 2019, www.pewsocialtrends.org/2017/12/05/on-gender-differences-no-consensus-on-nature-vs-nurture/.

48 Nehemiah 4:14.

49 John Eldredge, *Wild at Heart: Discovering the Secret of a Man's Soul* (New York: Thomas Nelson, 2001), Kindle.

50 D. C. McAllister, "My White Christmas in a Coal Mining Town, Circa 1975," *The Federalist*, December 20, 2014, thefederalist.com/2014/12/25/my-white-christmas-in-a-coal-mining-town-circa-1975/. Used with permission by the publisher.

51 D. C. McAllister, "Dads, Give Your Daughters the Gift of Football," *The Federalist*, December 17, 2014, thefederalist.com/2014/12/12/dads-give-your-daughters-the-gift-of-football/. Used with permission by the publisher.

52 Eldredge, *Wild at Heart.*

53 C. S. Lewis, *The Lion, the Witch and the Wardrobe* (London: HarperCollins, 2009).

54 Ibid, 66.

55 David Gilmore, *Manhood in the Making* (New Haven: Yale University, 1990), 35.

56 D. C. McAllister, "Today Let's Honor Men Instead of Making War Between the Sexes," *The Federalist*, March 8, 2017, thefederalist.com/2017/03/08/today-lets-honor-men-instead-making-war-sexes/. Used with permission by the publisher.

57 Levant and Kopecky, *Masculinity Reconstructed.*

58 Thomas A. Foster, *Sex and the Eighteenth Century Man: Massachusetts and This History of Sexuality in America* (Boston: Beacon Press, 2007), 68.

59 1 Corinthians 16:13–14.

60 Levant and Kopecky, Masculinity Reconstructed.

61 Ibid., 24.

62 Ibid., 27

63 Ibid., 44.
64 C. S. Lewis, *The Four Loves* (New York: First Mariner Books Edition, 2012), 218.
65 *Game of Thrones*, "Stormborn," Season 7 Episode 2. Directed by Mark Mylod. Written by Bryan Cogman (HBO, July 23, 2017).
66 Gilmore, *Manhood in the Making.*
67 Ibid., 203.
68 Ibid.
69 D. C. McAllister, "Navigating the Waters of a Broken Life: My Abortion Story," *The Federalist*, March 17, 2016, thefederalist.com/2014/06/19/navigating-the-waters-of-a-broken-life-my-abortion-story/. Used with permission by the publisher.
70 Moore and Gillette, King, Warrior, Magician, Lover, 122.
71 James Joyce, *A Portrait of the Artist as a Young Man* (New York: Dover Publications), Kindle, 48, 70–71.
72 James Joyce, Ulysses (Vigo Classics, 2011), iBooks, https://books.apple.com/us/book/ulysses/id765151079He.
73 Levant and Kopecky, *Masculinity Reconstructed*, 10–11.
74 Kelly Gilfillan, "Timeless Love Letters from the Civil War," Brentwood Home Page, February 12, 2015, brentwoodhomepage.com/timeless-love-letters-from-the-civil-war/.
75 Gail Collins, *America's Women: 400 Years of Dolls, Drudges, Helpmates, and Heroines* (New York: HarperCollins Publishers, 2009), 15.
76 Ibid.
77 Ibid., 17.
78 Ibid., 53.
79 Ibid., 54.

80 Ibid., 55.

81 Ibid.

82 Foster, *Sex and the Eighteenth Century Man*, 5.

83 Ibid., 10.

84 Ibid., 9–20.

85 Ibid., 25.

86 Ibid., 48.

87 Eldredge, *Wild at Heart*, 44.

88 Ibid.

89 George R. R. Martin, *Fire and Blood* (New York: Random House, 2018).

90 C. S. Lewis, *The Abolition of Man* (New York: HarperOne, 2009), iBooks, https://books.apple.com/us/book/the-abolition-of-man/id360635389.

91 Ibid.

92 George Orwell, *1984* (Classics To Go), iBooks, https://books.apple.com/us/book/1984/id1439686707.

93 David Carter, "Conscription for Women Displays the West's Death Wish," *The Federalist*, February 11, 2016, thefederalist.com/2016/02/11/conscripting-women-into-the-military-displays-the-wests-death-wish/.

94 Eddie Scarry, "Denise McAllister Tweets Weren't Homophobic, They Were Righteously Angry," *Washington Examiner*, April 1, 2019, https://www.washingtonexaminer.com/opinion/denise-mcallister-tweets-werent-homophobic-they-were-righteously-angry.

95 C. S. Lewis, Perelandra (*Space Trilogy #2*) (Distributed Proofreaders Canada, 2014), loc. 3349–3352, Kindle.

96 Jordan B. Peterson, *12 Rules for Life: An Antidote to Chaos* (Random House of Canada, 2018), Kindle, 190.

97 Lewis, *The Abolition of Man*.

98 Ibid.

99 Ibid.

100 Hannah Arendt, *The Origins of Totalitarianism* (New York: Penguin Classics, 2017).

NO LONGER PROPERTY OF
ANYTHINK LIBRARIES/
RANGEVIEW LIBRARY DISTRICT